Contents

Introduction

There is little doubt that the role and practices of social work continue to evolve and adapt in response to socio-cultural demands and socio-political expectations. Although there have been extraordinary changes in the lives of people and in the social, economic and physical environment in which they live, the social and cultural problems and economic difficulties that were endemic throughout the 20th century are still very much in evidence. Areas such as child neglect; domestic violence; killing of children by their parents/carers; physical, sexual, emotional and psychological abuse; poverty; homelessness; teenage pregnancies; youth crime; anti-social behaviour and drug and alcohol misuse continue to be causes of concern and their persistence blights the lives of many children and their families. These areas continue to be the focus of attention and intervention and there is a great deal of expectation and assumption about how the profession, and child care social workers in particular, should respond. Childcare social workers are at the sharp end of these concerns and they are expected to approach their duties as part of a multi-professional, multi-disciplinary and multi-agency team. As Gaynor Arnold, a social worker turned novelist, highlighted from her experience of social work ' . . . When I went back to "children and families" work five years later, I found a more structured world of priorities and time limits. There was far less preventative work, far more court work, far more young people with extreme behaviour and an explosion in the number of sexual abuse cases' (Arnold, 2009: 3).

Children and families social work is considered by social work practitioners, as well as people outside the profession, to be one of the most complex and difficult areas of social work practice. This is not to suggest that other areas of social work such as working with adults, people with learning difficulties, alcohol and substance misuse, mental health and people with impairment is not challenging. Indeed anyone with practice experience with any one of these groups would attest to the associated complexities and difficulties (as well as pleasures) involved. Having acknowledged the relative difficulties of working with various service user groups it is worth stating that there is something quite different about working with children and families that sets it apart from all other areas of social work. There is a heightened level of anxiety and scrutiny in this area of social work practice from which others

Social Control and the Use of Power in Social Work with Children and Families

Edited by

Toyin Okitikpi

Russell House Publishing

Russell House Publishing
First published in 2011 by:
Russell House Publishing Ltd.
4 St. George's House
Uplyme Road
Lyme Regis
Dorset DT7 3LS
Tel: 01297-443948
Fax: 01297-442722
e-mail: help@russellhouse.co.uk
www.russellhouse.co.uk

© Toyin Okitikpi and the various contributors
© Cover artwork Anna Lewis

British Library Cataloguing-in-publication Data:
A catalogue record for this book is available from the British Library

ISBN: 978-1-905541-71-3

Typeset by TW Typesetting, Plymouth, Devon
Printed by IQ Laser Press, Aldershot

About Russell House Publishing

Russell House Publishing aims to publish innovative and valuable materials to help
managers, practitioners, trainers, educators and students.

Our full catalogue covers: social policy, working with young people, helping children and
families, care of older people, social care, combating social exclusion, revitalising
communities and working with offenders.

Full details can be found at www.russellhouse.co.uk and we are pleased to send out
information to you by post. Our contact details are on this page.

We are always keen to receive feedback on publications and new ideas for future projects.

are spared. As well as having to work with vulnerable and at risks children/young people and their families, practitioners may also have to contend with aggressive, uncooperative, manipulative and untruthful parents and carers. The task of supporting and keeping children safe is further complicated by central government's ever changing priorities. There is continual introduction of, what some may describe as, bureaucratic systems and processes in an effort to improve practice and prevent further deaths and abuses. The pronouncements made about the profession by successive government ministers and the media has done little to engender public trust in the social work profession or the work that they do. The public are often baffled by why social services and social workers are unable to prevent children been abused or killed by their parents/carers. People's incredulity towards the profession is further compounded by the fact that many of the children killed or abused are generally known to social services as they are often already identified as in need of social work support and protection. Moreover they are usually assessed to be at risk of harm, and may already be on the at risk or child protection register.

The public's anger and negative perceptions about social workers is not assuaged in any sense by general acknowledgement that the profession faces a difficult and uphill struggle in their attempt to help and support families who do not want social workers involvement with their family. It could be argued that social work itself has done very little to make its case, to those outside the profession that it has been a force for good and has prevented far more abuse and deaths than is generally recognised. Rather than challenge the negative assumptions and misinformation about their work the profession has remained silent about the myriad of obstacles and problems that practitioners experience in trying to discharge their duties and safeguard children from being abused by their parents/carers. It is only since July 2009 that the profession and central government have taken the necessary initiatives to improve both the negative image that the public has of social work and social workers. It has already been documented, (Adams, Domielli and Payne, 2002; Horner, 2003; Okitikpi and Aymer, 2008) that while the nature and scope of social work is contested the practice of social work itself is pretty straightforward. At its heart social work practice is about building a working relationship with people in order to bring about change. It may seem an obvious point to make but people come to the attention of the social services for a reason. There are of course those who only seek information; ad hoc advice and provisions which social work could help them access. In effect these are not the groups that this publication is focusing on. Instead the focus is on the people that social work attempts to help and support so that they could better cope with, or deal adequately with, whatever difficulties they may be experiencing in their lives. It is during the process of working with these groups of service users that social workers may be called to exercise their legal responsibility and take draconian measures that may be deemed necessary.

In fear of power

It has already been acknowledged that children and families social work is one of the most difficult areas of social welfare practice. From the outset once attention has been drawn to the family because of concerns about a child the family would have to go through a level of scrutiny unbeknown by most families. The term initial assessment or investigation conveys a tone of neutrality and value free process. In reality, however sensitive and caring the professionals are in their approach, the experience for the family is not so benign. Families have to endure the presence of strangers probing into the minutia of their lives and are required to provide credible and verifiable explanations of events that led to a social worker contacting their family. The situation is not helped by the unspoken knowledge amongst those involved (families and professionals) that they are operating within an adversarial environment. Despite the reality, the impression generally given by the press to society at large is that all social workers are incompetent; poorly trained people who either take children into care unnecessarily or fail to act appropriately leaving children to suffer in the most appalling circumstances. Families who have been contacted because of child protection concerns may undergo emotional, psychological and, in some cases, physical pain. Despite their anger, fragility or unhappiness about the involvement of the agencies with their family they are still expected to cooperate with the authorities.

Although social workers have a range of powers that they can utilise in their day-to-day practice it is generally the case that they are often reluctant to make use of the full extent of these powers. There is a sense that practitioners view their role primarily as supporting children to stay within their social and familial environment. Indeed it could be argued that key legislation governing their practice supports this premise. Social workers appear, from the outside at least, to place a higher premium on keeping families together, at all cost, rather than (accommodating) taking children into care at the first opportunity. This is because accommodating children into care is not viewed as a good option with the possibility of a positive outcome. Instead it is seen as a last resort after all attempts to maintain or re-establish equilibrium or 'good-enough' parenting have been tried and failed. In essence rather than removing children from an abusive or poor nurturing environment in the first instance the situation is sometimes left to deteriorate beyond repair before any action is taken. Why this should be the case is of interest in this publication. Of course practitioners work within the parameters of the *Children Act (1989)* and the welfare threshold. However it is evident that local authorities operate at different levels with thresholds beyond which a child is deemed to be at risk of harm is set high in some authorities and higher still in others. It may be argued that the higher welfare threshold is further compounded by the fact that practitioners are uncomfortable being seen as over-zealous arbiters of draconian powers.

Children and families social work practitioners see themselves as sensitive, caring and non-judgemental people who are primarily concerned with the welfare of the children and their families. Cree and Davis' (2007) study reinforces the point that practitioners see their role as being that of an enabler and facilitator working alongside people. The entrenchment of user-involvement in all areas of the profession has also done much to reinforce practitioners' perception of the centrality of the caring aspects of their role.

The use of legal powers that distort the perception of social workers as an enabler and facilitator of change appears counter intuitive. Dominelli, (2002: 3) identified three different practice world view adopted by practitioners in the field. These approaches are characterised as:

- therapeutic helping approaches
- maintenance approaches
- emancipatory approaches

Similarly Cree and Myers, (2008: 2) highlight Payne's (2006) review of the profession of social work in which he characterised three views of social work thus:

1. Therapeutic views: social work is understood to be about 'seeking the best possible well-being for individuals, groups and communities, by promoting and facilitating growth and self fulfilment.
2. Transformational view: it is argued that social work must develop cooperation and mutual support in society so that the most oppressed and disadvantaged people can gain power over their own lives.
3. Social order view: social work is seen as an aspect of welfare services to individuals in societies. It meets individual's needs and improves services of which it is a part, so that social work and the services can operate more effectively.

Although both Dominelli (2002) and Payne (2006) each set out their different perspectives and approaches in social work however on close inspection it is evident that they are in fact both exploring and discussing the same areas. While there are practitioners whose approach is consistent with a particular perspective many practitioner are perhaps more pragmatic and would take, what could best be described as, an eclectic approach. For these practitioners their primary interest is to adopt whichever approach is most likely to achieve the desired outcome. However, in my view, despite these different approaches and perspectives that unites them all is the focus on care and support rather than control and the use of their powers.

The passage of time and subsequent changes in the socio-cultural and socio-political landscape has not completely decoupled social work from its historical influences (Cree and

Myers, 2008). Forged from philanthropic, religious (primarily Christian) and political (interestingly of the left, liberal and one-nation Toryism) background the profession has always seen itself as being partisan in favour of the poor and the dispossessed. It views itself as an advocate for the disenfranchised, the poor and those that are deemed to be on the margins of society. It does not see people as walking problems but rather as human beings with problems. Its starting point is that, for whatever reasons, people may experience a difficult period in their lives when they have to deal with situations and conditions that render them powerless and incapable of finding the appropriate solution without assistance. It recognises that although people do not always act in their own best interest and that sometimes people compound their problems by making the wrong choices this should not be used as justification for treating them unfairly and differently from everyone else in society. It could be argued that, in an effort not to appear to be judgemental about people's lifestyles and life choices, a culture has developed within social work whereby great latitude is afforded to many service users. For example, low level violence within families is ignored; poor school attendance is not seen as serious enough to act on; poor hygiene and lack of parental control is excused; drug and alcohol addiction are not by themselves seen as a cause for concern; a child growing up at home with a parent suffering from chronic mental health problem is not viewed to be vulnerable or at any particular risk. One of the explanations for such a relaxed attitude and lack of urgency is a combination of the rules of optimism and the unspoken belief that people who are victims of circumstance must be allowed to live their lives as they choose but with additional care and support. As such, practitioners should therefore not be judgemental or act unfairly by being 'control' led in their approach. The aim should therefore be to avoid further compounding people's situation or condition by assessing their parental capacity and capabilities using the same criteria as one would use for those outside the welfare system.

Increasing policing role

Social workers have always been viewed by some people, on the far left of the political spectrum, as part of the social problem because they are agents of the state. This perspective sees social workers' role as a sop for the poor and the marginalised by a brutal capitalist system. Although this view is not incorrect the difficulty with making such blanket statement is one of context, emphasis and the reality of individual experiences. It is the case that social workers operate within set criteria and clearly defined welfare thresholds and they are required, by law, to intervene where they have cause for concern. However, the argument being advanced is that trying to protect people from harm and preventing neglect and abuse should not be viewed as a negative or inconsequential endeavour.

For the first time in its history the profession is expected to play a far greater role in the policing of children's lives. However, the intriguing point is that societal expectations about a greater level of policing are implicit rather than explicit, although the controversial Vetting and Barring Procedures has changed the landscape dramatically. More than ever children and families social workers, in partnership with other professions, are required to exercise their powers more readily, while at the same time there is a great misgiving about practitioners being allowed to exert such powers. This particular point illustrates the contradiction that exists at the very heart of the duties and responsibilities placed on those working within the childcare field. In addition practitioners are not always going into passive environments where they are welcomed with open arms and a cup of tea and a biscuit. It is no longer unusual for practitioners to face intimidation, threats, verbal abuse, physical assault and malicious complaints.

The tension for practitioners in this climate is how to intervene earlier in order to prevent abuse and at the same time build rapport and develop the necessary relationship with the children and their families. In essence practitioners are expected to exercise their powers while at the same time not be discriminatory, judgmental or infringe on aspects of the human rights acts that relates to the children and their families'.

About this book

This is an edited book and its aim is to highlight the changing role of childcare social work and explore the complex nature of power and the use of power in social work in general and in the child care field in particular. As already mentioned although social work as a profession has always been about care and control, in reality practitioners are generally more comfortable with the care element of their role. Primarily social work believes in building a trusting relationship with services users and as a result they have always found the control aspect of their role problematic. Why there should be such a reluctance of social workers in England, Northern Ireland, Scotland and Wales to embrace the powers which have been vested in them is unclear, but there is evidence from social inquiry reports, (Maria Colwell; Jasmine Beckford; Thyra Henry; Victoria Climbe; Baby Peter) to suggest that practitioners, as a result of not exercising their powers, may have missed ample opportunities to act more decisively in order to prevent child abuse in general and child deaths in particular. While it is acknowledged that power is a far more complex concept than is general assumed; one of the tasks of this volume is to explore and reconsidered the nature and application of power in social work practice.

John Pitts (Chapter 1) provides a panoramic and historic overview of the social policy shift towards policing and enforcement in social welfare. At the beginning of his chapter explores how 'social control' is the processes by which individual and group behaviour is regulated in accordance with prevailing social norms, rules or laws. In his analysis social control is both internal and external; achieved by the introjection of the norms and values in early childhood, and the application of formal or informal sanctions or rewards in later life. Looking beyond just social workers' powers his analysis is full and detailed and takes account of governance and social control and, intriguingly, the criminalisation of social policy. Although his chapter focuses primarily on young people, youth work and the youth justice system, there is much however that would be of interest to general practitioners in the child care field.

Michael Preston-Shoot (Chapter 2) offers some critical reflections as well as an outline of the legal dimensions of social work with children and their families. He explores the nature and extent of practitioners powers and he casts an eye over the organisational context of social work practice and on the interface between law and ethics. He provides an analysis of various dualities and tensions within social work such as care versus control, needs versus resources, and professional autonomy versus employer direction.

Tom Wilks (Chapter 3) provides a critique of the application of traditional ethical frameworks to power. He discusses how power impinges on practice with children and families. He explores two key ethical frameworks and the ethics of care and their applicability to questions of how power operates in professional practice. He posits that acting ethically involves the interplay between principle and practice. Exploring social work and power, he notes that one of the ironies of social work practice is that the world outside of social work perceives social workers as powerful agents of the state whereas social workers themselves, describing their work, can sometimes lack a sense of power and agency in their day to day practice.

Julia Stroud (Chapter 4) explores child deaths and the socio-legal discourse of child protection. She also discusses how safeguarding considerations has been dominant in relation to child death. She highlights how Meta Analysis of serious case reviews are developing and shaping our knowledge and understanding of the circumstances surrounding child deaths. One of the interesting aspects of the chapter is her assertion that the interrogation of child death might be said to have been subsumed under the concept of fatal child abuse and the socio-legal discourse of safeguarding, however she contend that in fact, child death is rarely examined or reviewed in its entirety.

Toyin Okitikpi (Chapter 5) encourages the reformulation of the rule of optimism. In his exploration he suggests that social workers understanding of and use of power is bound up with their instinctive identification and support for service users. As a result power is viewed negatively and the use of power is seen as counterintuitive to their fundamental role as champions of the weak, the marginalised and the dispossessed.

Sarah Pond (Chapter 6) explored social workers' use of powers from a lay perspective. She provides a fresh and insightful analysis of the heavy emphasis placed upon supporting and respecting the views of clients without sufficiently acknowledging the protection role which social workers also carry. She opined that there are likely to be many occasions where social workers are placed in a 'no win' situation. She suggests that there is a need for some fundamental change which would allow social workers to continue to support vulnerable families but that they are in turn supported in making hard, tough decisions where those same families are at risk of causing harm.

Amanda Thorpe (Chapter 7) examines the notions of power, how social work practitioners use power in practice and the drivers and constraints involved in using the range of powers available to them. She considers the ways in which statutory powers may be used both to promote and undermine ethical practice. She looks at ideas of managerialism, de-professionalisation, reflexivity and reflective practice. She also considers social workers' understanding and application of the legal rules. She provides a framework to help ensure that practitioners use, as appropriate, the full extent of their statutory and professional powers to promote safe, ethical and anti-oppressive practice.

Andrew Brown (Chapter 8) examines the role of social workers in a school setting and explores the impact that their role could have on children, families and the school community. He looks at the implications for the practitioner in such settings and, drawing on his personal experiences, he puts forward practical ideas and suggestions that would be of interest to practitioners in such a setting. While he acknowledges that social workers in schools have limited powers, he suggests such limitations should not preclude them from acting and exerting a degree of control whenever necessary. He suggests that exercising power and control is possible -and is readily accepted in schools by parents – but it is how it is done that is crucial.

Akidi Ocan (Chapter 9) provides a detail account of social workers in the court arena. She highlights the point that social workers are often reluctant to use the Family Courts and the full range of their statutory powers in their efforts to safeguard children. She suggests social workers need to have a comprehensive knowledge of the extent of their powers and duties. In her view they also need to understand what is considered to be a lawful exercise of discretion and how and why the exercise of such discretion might be challenged in judicial review proceedings.

Jan Fook (Chapter 10) illustrates how critical reflection on assumptions about power (as embedded in the everyday practice of workers) can help forge a more complex and responsive practice. As well as a brief introduction to the theory and practice of critical reflection, particularly the notion of unearthing assumptions, she also considered the sorts of assumptions about power which are common in social work thinking. Finally she outlines how these conceptions of power might be reworked in a more complex way, through a critical reflection process.

References

Adams, R., Dominelli, L. and Payne, M. (Eds.) (2002) *Social Work: Themes, Issues and Critical Debates*. 2nd edn. Basingstoke, Palgrave/Macmillan.

Arnold, G. (2009) Stressful, Underpaid, and it's Downright Dangerous. *The Times.* May 8.

Cree, V. and Davis, A. (2007) *Social Work Voices from the Inside*. London, Routledge.

Cree, V. and Myers, S. (2008) *Social Work: Making a Difference*. Bristol, The Policy Press.

Dominelli, L. (2002) Anti-oppressive Practice in Context. In Adams, R., Dominelli, L. and Payne, M. (Eds.) (2002) *Social Work: Themes, Issues and Critical Debates*. 2nd edition. Basingstoke, Palgrave/Macmillan.

Horner, N. (2003) *What is Social Work? Context and Perspectives*. Exeter, Learning Matters.

Okitikpi, T. and Aymer, C. (Eds.) (2008) *The Art of Social Work Practice*. Lyme Regis, Russell House Publishing.

Payne, M. (2006) *What is Professional Social Work?* 2nd edn. Bristol, Policy Press.

Acknowledgements

I would like to say a special thank you to all the contributors to this volume. Despite their busy schedules they did not hesitate in their support to bring this publication into fruition. I am eternally grateful to Geoffrey Mann and the staff at Russell House whose support and encouragement is very much appreciated. Many thanks to Jayne Gould for her critical gaze over a number of the chapters and her encouraging words. I would also like to say a very special thanks to Debra, Rebecca, Joshua and now Reuben, the new addition to the family, for their unconditional love and support.

About the Editor and the Contributors

Toyin Okitikpi is a visiting Professor at University of Bedfordshire. Having started in residential care he qualified as a generic social worker and worked in the field for many years. His interest includes social work education; anti-discriminatory practice; the importance of education in the lives of children and young people; refugee and asylum seeking children and their families; social integration and cohesion; working with children of mixed parentage and, interracial/multicultural families and their experiences. He is a lay member on a number of Tribunals including: the General Medical Council's Fitness to Practice Panel; Nursing and Midwifery; Employment Tribunal; the Asylum and Immigration Tribunal and the Mental Health Review Tribunal. He has published on a number of social work related areas.

John Pitts is Vauxhall Professor of Socio-Legal Studies at the University of Bedfordshire. He is editor of *Safer Communities*, associate editor of *Youth and Policy* and an editorial board member of *Youth Justice* and *Juvenile Justice Worldwide* (UNESCO). His research includes studies of: The differential treatment of black and white young offenders; Anglo-French responses to youth crime and disorder; The violent victimisation of school students; Inter-racial youth violence; The impact of youth work with socially excluded young people in five European cities; The contribution of street-based youth work to the life chances of socially excluded young people in the UK and Violent youth gangs in three London boroughs.

Michael Preston-Shoot is Professor of Social Work and Dean of the Faculty of Health and Social Sciences at the University of Bedfordshire. He is a founding editor of the journal Ethics and Social Welfare, and an independent chair of both a local safeguarding children board and a safeguarding vulnerable adults board. He has researched and written widely on the interface between law and social work.

Tom Wilks is a Senior Lecturer in Social Work ad London South Bank University. He worked for many years as a social worker in a range of different settings. His research interests are in ethics, advocacy and service user involvement.

Dr Julia Stroud is a social work academic and Director of Social Work Studies at University of Brighton. She is a qualified and registered social worker. She has practised in both childcare and mental health settings and has extensive experience of statutory social work, particularly of child protection. Her research interests centre on child death, in particular on the relationship between mental disorder and child death. She is currently exploring safeguarding practices from a range of different theoretical perspectives.

Sarah Pond (MA) is a serving part-time board member with London Travel Watch and is a lay panellist for the General Medical Council. She is also a trustee of Hillingdon Carers and former Chair of a London Primary Care Trust, having spent her first 12 years of working life in the field of procurement in the private sector.

Amanda Thorpe is Principal Lecturer and Head of Social Work at the University of Bedfordshire with responsibility for the programmes leading to both qualifying and post qualifying awards in Social Work. Her particular teaching and research interests include anti-racist and anti-oppressive practice; the interface between social work law and practice; the teaching and assessment of law in qualifying social work education and reflective practice. Formerly an art teacher and later a Probation Officer, Amanda has experience of working in both the statutory and voluntary sectors with socially excluded and marginalised people, as well as with offenders in the community. She has a strong commitment to the principles of social justice which underpin her teaching and research.

Andrew Brown is a social worker based within an inner London Primary School. He has a great deal of experience in working with adults and young people in a variety of settings. He is interested in the practice of social work, in particular, direct and preventative work with children and families and young people.

Akidi Ocan has been a barrister since 1984 specialising in social services law including child protection, adult social care and mental health. Since 1990 she has represented local social services authorities in London and the South East. Akidi has trained practitioners in these areas of law extensively and she has regularly trained child protection social workers to improve their presentation in the courtroom. Akidi was appointed to the First-tier Tribunal in 2007 as a Tribunal Judge hearing appeals to the Mental Health Tribunal.

Jan Fook is Professor of Professional Practice Research and Director of the Interprofessional Institute with the South West London Academic Network (Royal Holloway, University of London, St Georges, University of London and Kingston University). Her work includes critical reflection, critical social work, professional practice and practice research. Her research work involves the empirical research of professional practice, and developing better methods for representing the complexity of this. A current interest is in developing critical reflection as a research method. She has published 13 books and over 70 book chapters and articles.

CHAPTER 1

Policy Shift – Towards Enforcement in Social Welfare

John Pitts

Social control

In the social sciences, the term 'social control' usually refers to the processes whereby individual and group behaviour is regulated in accordance with prevailing social norms, rules or laws. Whereas 18th century philosophers believed that the rapacious desires of 'men' could only be held in check by a strong State with the capacity to impose a 'a just measure of pain' (Ignatieff, 1978) later thinkers, like Freud (1965) and Meszaros (1972) granted primacy to early childhood socialisation; the inculcation of the prohibitions and taboos that are the precondition for social life.

The modern State pursues both strategies, supporting the inculcation of social control via its child welfare policies while endeavouring to contain social deviance through its criminal justice policies. However social control is never either absolute or neutral. As Freud (1931) observed, the struggle between socialisation and desire, the ego and the id, is perennial while, as Habermas (1975) notes, the validity of the norms, values, rules and laws to which conformity is required, not to mention the legitimacy of the agencies and organisations requiring conformity, are a perennial subject of contestation.

Governance and social control

Whereas Conservatives have tended to accept traditional modes of social control fairly uncritically: not so progressives and radicals. Until the 1960s, left-wing intellectuals were primarily concerned with the ways in which the normal mechanisms of social control compounded class inequality (c.f. Willis, 1973). From the 1960s, however, the politics of class was supplanted by a new politics of identity which implicated these same mechanisms in the subjugation of women, ethnic minorities and non-heterosexuals (Greer, 1973).

The oil crisis of the 1970s and the slow demise of the Soviet Union in the 1970s and 1980s, paralleled the eclipse of the, 'modernist', 'grand narratives' of Marxism, Fabianism and Keynsian Economics (Booker, 1980) that had given meaning to the politics of the post-war era. In their place emerged a new, disparate, assortment of ideas that came to be called 'post-modernism' (Lyotard, 1993). Terry Eagleton (2003) has observed that the emergence of post-modernism marked a moment of crisis on the political Left, noting that, having abandoned the old story about the inexorable forward march of the proletariat, the Left now seemed prepared to settle for 'any old story'. Whereas modernism was associated with ideas of social progress and political unity, for postmodernism ideas like 'progress' 'unity', 'feminism', 'socialism' or racial or gender equality were just 'discourses', 'texts', 'signifiers' with no necessary counterpart in the 'reality'. Post modernism had two major preoccupations; power (bad) and bodies, particularly desiring bodies, (good). As a result, a great deal of intellectual energy went into discovering how power was utilised to exert social control over bodies. In the fullness of time this was to spawn a debate about what Stephen Rose (1999) called the 'governance of souls'.

'Governance', social control and young people

The 'governance thesis', locates the impetus to govern in a generalised, Nietzschean, 'will to power', and the subject of governance as a product and tool of 'governmentality' (Merquoir, 1985). In this perspective, the governance of the young becomes politically important in 'post-traditional', (Giddens 1999) 'advanced liberal' (Rose, 1999) 'late modern' (Garland, 2001) or 'post-modern' (Lyotard, 1993) societies because of the State's need to establish or sustain its political authority in a situation where its capacity to govern directly has been substantially eroded (Rose, 1999).

Whereas, on the one hand, economic globalisation has limited the capacity of the nation state to intervene effectively in economic life, on the other, the waning of traditional social divisions has served to release individuals from the '*conscience collective*' of class, family, race and gender, requiring them to assume unprecedented authorship of their own lives. Thus, they must effect new choices and assume new responsibilities in the spheres of employment, education, personal relationships, location, leisure and lifestyle which, in a traditional society, were determined in large part by socialisation, culture and social structure and serviced by an interventionist state. There is simply less for government to do, even as the society it would govern becomes ever more diverse and divergent (Young, 1999).

Whereas in the heyday of the welfare state, it is argued, governments endeavoured to ameliorate the depredations of the capitalist market by direct intervention in the social and economic spheres, now, spheres of activity previously dominated by government; health, education, policing, public transport etc., are ceded to the market. Rose characterises this shift as the 'death of the social', a process in which the welfare state, relinquishes its role as a universal safety net for the citizen. Now, Rose (1996) argues, particular 'communities', not 'society', become the focus of social and criminal justice policy.

Eagleton tells of a literary conference in the 1970s at which a, not atypical, paper entitled *Let's Put the Anus Back into Coriolanus* was presented without apparent irony.

This is necessary, the argument runs, because the disruption caused in these neighbour-hoods and amongst these populations by the withdrawal of the state during a period of accelerated social transformation and heightened uncertainty threatens to undermine its political authority, thus fostering dissent and social disorder. In these circumstances, it is argued, government must galvanise a constituency and devise forms of 'governance', that will allow it to re-establish the political authority, and hence the social control it was able to exert when it was able to 'govern' directly.

It achieves this, the argument goes, by directing the anxieties generated by accelerating social, economic and cultural change, via a process of 'populist ventriloquism' (Matthews, 2005) towards certain categories of demonised 'other', against whom governments then act. In what Ulrich Beck (1992) characterises as the 'risk society', it is the anxieties, rather than the ideals, of electors and those who wish to be elected by them that drive the political process. Moreover, in a situation where the voters who make the difference are, disproportionately, middle-aged, white and relatively prosperous, it comes as no surprise, the argument runs, that the targets of governmental demonisation, and this new form of governance, are disproportionately non-white, non-prosperous and young (Pitts, 2003). Hence, as David Garland (2001) argues, the demise of 'the solidarity project' is paralleled by the emergence of a 'culture of control'.

In their attempts to conceptualise contemporary policies directed at, and professional practice with, needy, 'socially excluded' and offending children and young people, both critical and mainstream criminologists have converged upon the notion of 'youth govern-ance'. The term has come to serve as a catchall characterisation of, and explanation for, a broad range of governmental and quasi-governmental interventions with children and young people, spanning child protection, education, crime prevention and incarceration.

> *What is less open to dispute is the diverse and expanding array of strategies that is available to achieve the governance of young people. It is an array that is capable of drawing in the criminal and the non-criminal, the deprived and the depraved, the neglected and the dangerous . . . Youth is largely defined in terms of what is lacking rather than by what it is. This is one reason why young people are afforded a central place in law and order discourse. They remain the touchstone through which crime and punishment can be imagined and re-imagined. Simon (1997) has argued that the salience*

of law and order in the United States is such that its citizens are continually governing themselves through their reaction to crime. Arguably, more accurately, it is the constellation of images thrown up by youth, disorder and crime that provide the basis of contemporary contexts of governance.

Muncie and Hughes, 2002: 13

However, as Roger Matthews (2005) notes:

While Jonathon Simon was writing his widely referenced book 'Governing Through Crime' (2007) the issue of crime was rapidly dropping down the public and political agenda. Indeed, there are signs that as the crime rate drops and attention turns increasingly to the wider issues of security and anti-social behaviour, we are moving into a 'pre-crime' society where the aim is to prevent crime rather than 'cracking down' on it.

Nonetheless, Nikolas Rose's (1999) now familiar complaint that 'childhood is the most intensively governed sector of personal existence' continues to elicit academic support. Thus John Muncie and Gordon Hughes (2002: 2) contend that:

Since child offenders were first tentatively separated from adults in youth prisons and subsequently in reformatories, discourses of youth and childhood have emphasised not only indiscipline but also vulnerability. Both constructions have legitimated innumerable programmes designed to mould and shape child development whether by coercion or seduction, education and persuasion. The casting of children as in need of guidance and support has enabled virtually every aspect of childhood development to be subject to regulation, surveillance and inspection.

This is undoubtedly true. Children are prohibited by the state from quaffing whiskey from bottles in the street, working up chimneys or owning firearms. They can be removed from their homes against their will if one of their parents is a known paedophile, made to go to school and, post-*Jamie's School Dinners*, even prevented from eating mechanically reclaimed meat products whilst they are there. But is this so surprising? As every parent knows, not least of the reasons that childhood is so 'intensively governed' is that children and young people really are more vulnerable and less able to protect themselves than adults and may, from time to time, need adults, or indeed the state, to intervene to protect them.

This blanket repudiation of state intervention has its origins in the blanket repudiation within post-modernism of 'power ' in general and social norms in particular; the vehicles *par excellence* for the 'normalising' discourses wherein the state accomplishes its 'governance of souls' (Rose, 1999). Yet, as Terry Eagleton has argued:

It is a mistake to believe that norms are always restrictive. In fact it is a crass romantic delusion. It is normative in our kind of society . . . that child murderers are punished, that

4

working men and women may withdraw their labour, and that ambulances speeding to a traffic accident should not be impeded just for the hell of it. Anyone who feels oppressed by all this must be seriously oversensitive. Only an intellectual who has overdosed on abstraction could be dim enough to imagine that whatever bends a norm is politically radical.

Eagleton, 2003: 15

For the champions of the youth governance thesis, however, all state action vis-à-vis children and young people represent an unwarranted intrusion in their lives. There is no notion here that educational, health and welfare services may actually benefit their recipients, nor that the state may be composed of contradictory elements, a 'right' hand and a 'left' hand (Bourdieu, 1998) and that, in some degree, these services may be the fruit of earlier working class struggles which should, one might have thought, be defended, rather than decimated.

Using such an elastic concept as 'youth governance' while suggesting that it is a product of the crisis confronting the state in 'late modernity' presents two problems. Firstly, it obscures as much as it explains, leading us to assume that what are actually divergent or contradictory tendencies within state policy are mere instances of a single phenomenon. Secondly, it overstates the break with the past that 'youth governance' is supposed to represent by arguing that the present era is distinctive in terms of the anxieties of those who govern and the objectives and forms of governance they are constrained to adopt.

The ostensible concerns of contemporary family and youth policy; the widening gap between the 'haves' and 'have-nots' (*Tax Credits, Urban Regeneration*) the capacity of the lower class family to offer adequate parenting (*Sure Start, Youth Inclusion and Support Panels* [*YISPs*] *Parenting Orders*) the attitudinal, physical and technical preparedness of the young to enter education, training and employment (*Education Action Zones, Connexions, Offending Programmes*) the threat to social order (*The New Youth Justice, Community Safety Partnerships, ASBOs*) and social and political cohesion (*Active Communities, Citizenship Education, Restorative Justice*) have been central to the major developments in family policy, education, youth work and youth justice throughout the 20th century. Moreover, as is the case today, these concerns, and these developments, have tended to emerge during periods of rapid social and economic change and heightened social anxiety (Pitts, 1988).

The final decades of the 19th century saw widespread political and media concern about the perceived 'crisis of control' in the industrial cities (Pearson, 1983) and the apparent ineffectiveness of the justice system and other agencies of control (Garland, 1985). This crisis was seen to be a product of the effects of economic recession upon the capacity of the lower class family to exert sufficient control over its children. Alongside this were related concerns about the academic and physical fitness of British youth for military service and their capacity to resist the blandishments of a newly ascendant Bolshevism, as well as religious and philanthropic concerns about the suffering of lower class children and young people. These concerns triggered the proliferation of uniformed youth organisations and 'street' and club-based youth work (Kaufman, 2001) radical educational reform, in the shape of Balfour's *1902 Education Act*, which brought Local Education Authorities into being, and the introduction of a new youth justice system by the Asquith administration in 1908 (Newburn, 1995).

From the late 1950s, concerns about growing social inequality (Abel-Smith and Townsend, 1965) rising crime and disorder, political disengagement amongst the young, the employability of low-achieving working class children and a perceived decline in the quality of lower class parenting, precipitated a national poverty programme (The Community Development Projects) further expansion of 'street' and club-based youth work (Albemarle, 1960) radical welfare reform (the *Children and Young Persons Act, 1963*) educational reform culminating in comprehensive education and a raised school leaving age (the Newsom Report, *Half Our Future*, 1961) and the introduction of a new youth justice system by the Wilson administration (the *Children in Trouble* White Paper and the *Children and Young Person's Act, 1969*).

Then, as now, it was 'modernising' governments that triggered this intensification of intervention with lower class children and young people and, then as now, these governments argued that their new measures were 'evidence-based'; being informed by the new sciences of paediatrics, child psychology, social administration, sociology, criminology and penology. Then, as now, they attracted the enthusiastic legitimation of academics and, then as now, this intensification of intervention with lower class children and young people led to the simultaneous expansion of youth work, social work and youth justice, generating both heightened levels of 'social education' (Davies and Gibson, 1967) and greater incarceration and community surveillance (Garland, 1985; Pitts, 1988; Newburn, 1995).

New Labour's youth service

The election of a Labour government in 1997 witnessed an attempt to develop a coherent youth policy through the appointment of a Minister for Youth, the establishment of a dedicated Cabinet Committee for Young People and an Inter-Departmental Children and Young People's Unit in 2001. The political importance ascribed to the 'youth question' by New Labour is evidenced by an apparently unending stream of policies concerned with the capacity of young people to make a successful transition to a self-sufficient law-abiding adulthood (Coles, 2000; Mizen, 2003). Moreover, these policies echoed many of the concerns, and embodied many of the changes, for which radical professionals and academics in the fields of youth work, youth justice, education, child welfare, policing and drug treatment had been campaigning for almost 30 years (Jeffs, 1979). This unprecedented investment was a response to governmental anxieties that, left unaddressed, the social consequences of the profound social and economic changes occurring in the UK in the preceding twenty years: structural, trans-generational, unemployment, family breakdown, and widening social and economic polarisation, resulting in heightened levels of crime and disorder amongst the most disadvantaged, would lead to the erosion of social cohesion and social control (Social Exclusion Unit, 1998).

These policies and the extra investment they generated have created a new, expanded, market in youth services, attracting many non-traditional, service providers into the sector. A study of street-based youth work, undertaken by the present author and his colleagues between 2001 and 2003 (Crimmens et al., 2004) identified 1,547 projects. This represented a 15 fold increase over the mid-1970s (Marks, 1976) the period before government cutbacks led to the contraction of youth service provision and the decimation of street-based youth work. That the bulk of this growth has occurred under New Labour is attested to by the fact that just over half of the 564 projects returning questionnaires had been operating for three years or less, with almost a quarter having been in operation for under one year.

What is different is that contemporary street-based youth work tends to be time-limited, problem-oriented and 'target-driven', concerned, for example, with employability, youth crime prevention, substance abuse, sexual health, teenage pregnancy, youth homelessness, truancy and school exclusion. It employs workers from health, welfare, urban re-generation, education and criminal justice agencies. As such it has adopted a markedly different emphasis and a different ethos from the user-led, social-educational approaches developed within mainstream youth work over the preceding 45 years (Davies and Gibson, 1967; Jeffs and Smith, 2002).

This changed emphasis is part of a broader reconfiguration of the welfare state in which social policy is supposed to 'buttress rather than burden the wealth producing economy' (Taylor-Gooby, 2003). In this shift from the 'welfare state' of old to a new 'social investment state' (Fawcett et al.) the eradication of dependency and the promotion of future employability becomes a central rationale for state expenditure upon children and young people. Thus, investment in pre-school education, reducing teenage pregnancy or social crime prevention is justified on the grounds that it will not only obviate the future costs of school failure, welfare dependency and crime, but it will also foster employability. This is why, across the sector, in education, training, youth work, youth crime prevention and youth justice we see such a huge emphasis upon the eradication of supposedly self-defeating behaviours and attitudes; upon understanding the consequences of one's actions for oneself and others and the acquisition and accreditation of the life, social, educational and vocational skills which will, it is argued, facilitate a successful transition to the labour market.

While this reconfiguration of youth services may not represent the 'death of the social' it does betoken a further shift from universalism towards targeting services at particular, problematic, populations? Whether this marks such a significant break with the past as is sometimes claimed however is debatable. In reality, Albemarle's (1960) dream of a universal youth service had effectively run out of steam by the early 1970s (Factor and Pitts, 2001). Despite consistent demands from youth and community workers, their trades unions and the voluntary sector, that the reach and the brief of the youth service be expanded to incorporate concerns about vocational training, employment and political and welfare rights, and that young people's interests should be represented in government at ministerial level, nothing was done about these issues until the election of the first Blair administration.

New Labour's new youth justice

The youth justice system introduced by the first Blair administration (Pitts, 2003) was rooted in a repudiation of what we might call, for the sake of convenience, the 'old youth justice'. The old youth justice comprised 1960/70s 'welfarism', which emphasised the central role of social inequality in the aetiology of youth offending and the need for robust state intervention to ameliorate their personal and social circumstances, and 1970s/80s 'progress-ive minimalism' which strove to divert young people from a potentially stigmatising formal involvement in the justice system.

In the 'new youth justice' these apparently contradictory ideas were supplanted by a focus upon the deeds rather than the needs of young offenders, unless these needs could be shown to have led directly to their offending, and a strategy of early, and in some cases pre-emptive, formal intervention with crime-prone and offending young people (Pitts, 2003). These interventions were rooted in the belief that early exposure to the system will have long-term deterrent and rehabilitative effects. However, because the elements which comprised the 'new youth justice' were assembled with an eye to how the proposed changes would play in the Tory heartlands rather than their 'systemic effects', and because New Labour ministers were more receptive to the good news offered by their inexperienced political advisers than the misgivings of civil servants, justice system professionals and academics, they failed to spot that the new system's plumbing was awry and that it was therefore destined to draw in many relatively unproblematic young people and to accelerate their progress through the system and into security or custody (Pitts, 2003; Kemp et al., 2003).

The Crime and Disorder Act (1998) increased the number of offences for which juveniles could be imprisoned, increased sentence lengths, extended the 'grave crimes' provisions (i.e. offences which in the case of an adult would attract a maximum sentence of 15 years) to children of 10, extended the powers of youth courts to remand children and young people directly into secure and penal establishments, introduced 'fast-tracking' for persistent young offenders and lowered the age at which young people in trouble could be incarcerated. It also abandoned specific 'community alternatives to custody'. Thus, between 1992 and 2002 the numbers of children and young people aged 10–17 sentenced to security or custody in England and Wales rose by 80 per cent. In 2002/3 12,592 children and young people entered Young Offender Institutions, Local Authority Secure Units (LASUs) and Secure Training Centres (STCs) (Youth Justice Board, 2005). Moreover, in the decade 1992–2002, the numbers of under-15s held in security or custody increased by, a remarkable, 800 per cent (Bateman and Pitts, 2005). However, during this time, crimes recorded as having been committed by children and young people fell by 20 per cent (Bateman and Pitts, 2005).

Some UK commentators have argued that this burgeoning youth custody population did not wholly displease sentencers and a government which achieved office, in part at least, by wresting the mantle of 'law and order' from the Conservative party (Pitts, 2003). In his highly influential *Culture of Control* (2001) David Garland argues that in 'Anglo-America' in the recent period, we have witnessed the decline of the rehabilitative ideal, a renewed emphasis upon punitive sanctions, dramatic changes in the emotional tone of criminal justice policy and the emergence of a 'penal populism' in which the 'victim' becomes the central focus of criminal justice policy.

There certainly appears to be plenty of evidence that the justice system in general and the youth justice system in particular has got tougher under New Labour. With 108.2 prisoners for every 100,000 of the population, the justice system of England and Wales appears to be the most punitive in Europe (Kommer, 2004). However, when we compare prison numbers with convictions and arrests for serious offences across Europe, England and Wales emerges as a significantly less punitive country than raw imprisonment rates would suggest (Kommer, 2004). Indeed, it appears that some, at least, of the increase in secure and custodial numbers is attributable to the increased seriousness of youth crime. As crime rates in general have fallen, arrests for sexual offences and serious, violent, gun-related, drug-related and drug-driven crime have risen. In 2002/3, arrests for sexual offences rose 15 per cent, arrests for drug-related offences 12 per cent and arrests for violence against the person rose 9 per cent. Although between 1992 and 2002 the numbers of children and young people entering the courts remained fairly constant, the proportion of defendants sentenced to custody rose from 44 per cent to 63 per cent (Home Office, 2003). Yet, Youth Court magistrates interviewed by Burnett and Appleton (2004) were adamant that their sentencing had grown no more severe over the period and that custodial sentences were only imposed when absolutely necessary. While it is true that the government extended the 'grave crimes' provision from 15 to 12 year olds, thus drawing a handful of younger children into the Crown

Court for sentencing, between 1992 and 2002 the numbers of children and young people remitted to Crown Court for sentencing, because the seriousness of their offences appeared to merit a more severe penalty than the Youth Court was able to impose, rose by 30 per cent (Home Office, 2003). While some of this increase may be attributable to a toughening of the system it is unlikely that all of it is.

Political responses have been ambivalent and sometimes contradictory, as politicians have faced the challenge of developing a youth crime strategy equal to the complexity of the problems of youth crime and disorder currently confronting the UK. The fact that UK politicians talk, and sometimes act, 'tough' on youth crime may be obscuring the reality that, in 1998, New Labour ministers actually believed that, over time, the raft of child and youth focused social initiatives they were introducing and the new 'evidence-based' youth justice system they had brought into being would reduce the numbers entering the system and 'turn around' the remaining few who did. The architects of the act presumed that the proven efficacy of the 'evidence-based' programmes which underpin these penalties would ensure that only a handful of the most intractable offenders would persist beyond this stage. Indeed the whole logic of the 1998 Act is predicated upon the success of these measures. In its original conception the new community penalties were to be the means whereby custody would be averted and the juvenile custodial population reduced (Pitts, 2003).

While the liberal critique of contemporary youth justice policy points to a straightforward determination on the part of governments in both North America and the UK to impose draconian penalties upon young offenders (Garland, 2001) the reality is more complex. Unlike the USA, in the UK in the recent past ever more rights have been granted to juvenile and adult subjects of justice systems. In 1990, unlike the USA, the UK government signed the *UN Convention on the Rights of the Child* and although, the recent UN Committee report finds the UK wanting in its treatment of young offenders the UK government has nonetheless committed itself to this humanitarian benchmark against which its actions may be judged (United Nations, 2002). The *Human Rights Act* (1998) which incorporated many of the provisions of the *European Convention on Human Rights* into English Law reinforced this commitment. The first Prisons Ombudsman was appointed in the mid-1990s and an eminent penal reformer has recently filled the role of Chief Inspector of Prisons. In the Secure Training Centres, introduced by the 1998 Act, elaborate arrangements for independent inspection and institutional transparency were instituted. Yet in 2003, a judicial review ruled that the provisions of the *Children Act* (1989) should apply to Prison Department Young Offender Institutions, thus posing a challenge to the Home Office Prison Department and the Youth Justice Board of England and Wales. Thus, while in 2002 the Prime Minister, the Home Secretary the Chair of the Youth Justice Board and the Lord Chief Justice all called for tougher custodial penalties for particular categories of young offenders, they have also bemoaned the rising level of youth incarceration and introduced measures, such as the Intensive Supervision and Surveillance Programmes (ISSPs) in an attempt to reverse the situation.

In 2008, the widely criticised 'sanction detection' Key Performance Indicator (KPI) imposed upon the police by government earlier in the decade was abandoned and replaced by a KPI concerned with reducing the number of first time entrants to the youth justice system. This rediscovery of 'diversion' had an instant and dramatic effect upon the numbers of children and young people entering the system per se but also upon the numbers entering custody. This is a policy shift which is occurring not only in the UK but also in the USA, following a three decade long carceral bonanza (Austin et al., 1999; Blumstein and Beck, 1999; Pitts, 2010). This swing of the penal pendulum, back towards non-intervention and decarceration (Bernard, 1992) is supported by evidence that most first time entrants would have desisted from crime of their own accord and that incarceration tends to compound nascent criminal careers. However, it is almost certainly prompted by dwindling policing and youth justice budgets.

The criminalisation of social policy

The criminalisation of social policy concerns the justification of policies in the spheres of education, training, social welfare etc. on the basis of their purported contribution to crime control. This involves the incorporation of previously autonomous educational, training, or social welfare services, agencies or organisations, in whole or in part, into the crime the control apparatus. It also involves the adoption by crime control agencies of techniques originally developed within education, training, or social welfare.

The adoption of a 'social investment' rationale for social and criminal justice policies targeting young people has meant that, over the past decade, the dividing line between the criminal justice apparatus and education, employment and social welfare services has become ever more blurred. The rationale for this integration of services is, of course, that because youth crime, disorder and social exclusion are inextricably linked, responses must also be 'joined-up'. Integration is achieved, in part, by re-configured funding regimes that require the plethora of would-be providers, drawn into the youth services market by the proliferation of government initiatives, to bid for tightly specified, time-limited contracts. The extent to which these changed funding regimes have enabled government to determine the foci of interventions is evidenced by recent shifts in the targeting of street-based youth work. Comparing street-based youth work projects surveyed in 2002 with those surveyed in 1999 (Skinner, 1999) we see a sharp decline in 'universal', area-based, work targeting the generality of young people in an identified geographical area, and the proliferation of issues-based work targeting particular types of problems, or groups and individuals deemed to be 'at risk' in some way (Crimmens et al., 2004).

On the face of it, this gives central government substantially increased power to shape, policy, strategy and professional practice at local level. Under the influence of the Home Office, New Labour has endeavoured to assign an increasingly central role in the prevention and control of youth crime and disorder to educational, employment, welfare and youth services and the multi-agency partnership, with its attendant funding streams, has been a vehicle for the achievement of this objective.

However, the national street-based youth work study, referred to above, revealed that these pressures towards 'institutional criminalisation' played out quite differently in different areas. Thus, we found areas where the police have taken to faxing details of 'disorder hotspots' and lists of suspected perpetrators to the youth service HQ in the expectation that workers would use this information to target their work. On the other hand, we found instances in which partnership working enabled the effective de-criminalisation of youthful offending. In the YJB-funded Youth Inclusion Programme (YIP) one of 11 projects studied in depth by the research team, staff worked on a broad range of non-crime-related issues with 150 or so 'hard-to-reach' young people in the broader social networks and friendship groups of the 50 young people formally targeted by the YIP partners. This meant that they received a youth work service where none had existed before. The workers understood client-worker confidentiality with this group of youngsters to mean that their identities would not be shared with other partnership agencies. For their part these agencies, the police, education, social services, accepted this as a necessary and potentially productive strategy.

Unless they take place within the youth justice system, interventions with hard-to-reach young people are inevitably shaped in crucial ways by the day-to-day, face-to-face, interaction between workers and young people. Seventy seven per cent of the 564 projects surveyed in the national study claimed that all their work was negotiated with the young people while the other 23 per cent said that they introduced 'some curriculum elements'. 65 per cent of the 102 young people interviewed about the worker's role and their own, said that they plan and decide things with the workers while a further 28 per cent said that the workers usually did what the young people asked them to do. They also maintained that their involvement with these workers had enabled them to achieve goals they, rather than the workers, had defined.

Conclusion

While it is true that the past two decades have witnessed attempts by government to exert greater social control over young people via youth work and the youth justice system, it appears that in both cases their efforts have met with resistance. In the case of youth work, it has proved exceptionally difficult to engage young people in narrowly defined interventions around particular problems and, in most cases, workers have found it necessary to broaden and democratise their approach by responding to the stated needs and wishes of the young people they wish to engage. In the case of the youth justice system, the lack of effectiveness of the elaborate forms of intervention ushered in by the *Crime and Disorder Act* (1998) combined with a changing orientation in Anglophone youth justice systems towards 'diversion', prompted in no small part by fiscal constraints, appears to be leading to a less interventionist and less punitive policies.

References

Abel-Smith, B. and Townsend, P. (1965) *The Poor and the Poorest*. London, Bell and Sons.

Albemarle Report (1960) *On the Youth Service in England and Wales*. London, HMSO.

Austin, J., Clark, J., Hardyman, P. and Henry, D. (1999) The Impact of Three Strokes and You're Out. *Punishment and Society*, I: 131–62.

Bateman, T. and Pitts, J. (Eds.) (2005) *The Russell House Companion to Youth Justice*. Lyme Regis, Russell House Publishing.

Beck, U. (1992) *The Risk Society: Towards a New Modernity*. London, Sage.

Bernard, T. (1992) *The Cycle of Juvenile Justice*. Oxford, Oxford University Press.

Bernard, T.J. (1992) *The Cycle of Juvenile Justice*. New York, Oxford University Press.

Blumstein, A. and Beck, A.J. (1999) Population Growth in US Prisons, 1980–1996. In Tonry, M. and Petersilia, J. (Eds.) *Crime and Justice: A Review of the Research, Vol. 26*. Chicago, IL: University of Chicago Press.

Booker, C. (1980) *The Seventies*. Harmondsworth, Penguin.

Bourdieu, P. (1998) *Acts of Resistance*. Cambridge, Polity Press.

Burnett, R. and Appleton, C. (2004) *Joined-up Youth Justice: Tackling Youth Crime in Partnership*. Lyme Regis, Russell House Publishing.

Coles, B. (2000) Slouching Towards Bethlehem: Youth Policy and the Work of the Social Exclusion Unit. In Hartley, D. Sykes, R. and Woods, R. *Social Policy Review* (12). London, Social Policy Association.

Crimmens, D., Factor, F., Jeffs, T., Pitts J., Spence, J., Pugh, C. and Turner, P. (2004) *Reaching Socially Excluded Young People: A National Study of Street-based Youth Work*. Leicester/York, National Youth Agency/Joseph Rowntree Foundation.

Davies, B. and Gibson, A. (1967) *The Social Education of the Adolescent*. London, University of London Press.

Eagleton, T. (2003) *After Theory*. London, Allen Lane.

Factor, F. and Pitts, J. (2001) From Emancipation to Correctionalism: UK Youth Work and the Politics of the Third Way. In Puuronen, V. *Youth on the Threshold of the Third Millenium*, Joensuu Finland, Joensuu University Press.

Fawcett, B., Featherstone, B. and Goddard, J. (2004) *Contemporary Child Care Policy and Practice*. Basingstoke, Palgrave.

Freud, S. (1930) *Civilization and Its Discontents*. London, Hogarth.

Freud, S., Strachey, J. and Gay, P. (1965) *New Introductory Lectures on Psychoanalysis*, London, W.W. Norton and Company.

Garland, D. (1985) *Punishment and Welfare, A History of Penal Strategies*. London, Gower.

Garland, D. (2001) *Culture of Control*. Oxford, Oxford University Press.

Giddens, A. (1999) *The Third Way: The Renewal of Social Democracy*. Cambridge, Polity Press.

Greer, G. (1970) *The Female Eunuch*. Harmondsworth, Penguin.

Habermas, J. (1976) *Legitimation Crisis*. London, Heinemann Educational Books.

Home Office (2003) *Criminal Statistics England and Wales*. Norwich, HMSO.

Ignatieff, M. (1978) *A Just Measure of Pain: The Penitentiary in The Industrial Revolution*. London, Pantheon.

Jeffs, T. (1979) *Young People and the Youth Service*. London, Routledge and Kegan Paul.

Jeffs, T. and Smith, M. (2002) Individualisation and Youth Work. *Youth and Policy*, 76.

Kaufman, S. (2001) Detached Youth Work. In Factor, F., Chauhan, V. and Pitts, J. (Eds.) *The Russell House Companion to Working with Young People*. Lyme Regis, Russell House Publishing.

Kemp. V., Sorsby. A., Liddle. M. and Merrington. S. (2003) *Assessing Responses to Youth Offending in Northamptonshire*. NACRO Research Briefing 2, London, Nacro.

Kommer, G. (2004) Punitiveness in Europe Revisited. *Criminology in Europe*, 3: 1, Feb.

Lyotard, J-F. (1979) *The Post Modern Condition*. Manchester, Manchester University Press.

Marks, K. (1976) *Detached Youth Work Practice in the Mid-Seventies*, Occasional Paper 18, Leicester, National Youth Bureau.

Matthews, R. (2005) The Myth of Punitiveness. *Theoretical Criminology*, 9: 2, 175–201.

Merquoir, J. (1985) *Foucault*. London, Fontana Press.

Meszaros, I. (1972) *The Necessity of Social Control*. London, Merlin Press.

Mizen, P. (2003) Tomorrow's Future or Signs of a Misspent Youth, *Youth and Policy*, 79.

Muncie, J. and Hughes, G. (2002) Modes of Youth Governance, Political Rationalities, Criminalisation and Resistance. In Muncie, J. and Hughes, G. *Youth Justice: Critical Readings*. London, Sage.

Muncie, J. and Hughes, G. (2002) Modes of Youth Governance, Political Rationalities, Criminalisation and Resistance. In Muncie, J. and Hughes, G. *Youth Justice: Critical Readings*. London, Sage.

Newburn, T. (1995) *Crime and Criminal Justice Policy.* London, Longman.

Pearson, G. (1983) *Hooligan: A History of Respectable Fears.* Basingstoke, Macmillan.

Pease, K. (1994) Cross National Imprisonment Rates. In King, R. and Maguire, M. (Eds.) *Prisons in Context.* Oxford, Clarendon Press.

Pitts, J. (1988) *The Politics of Juvenile Crime.* London, Sage.

Pitts, J. (2003) Changing Youth Justice. *Youth Justice,* 3: 1, 5–20.

Pitts, J. (2003) *The New Politics of Youth Crime: Discipline or Solidarity.* Lyme Regis, Russell House Publishing.

Rose, N. (1996) The Death of the Social? Re-figuring the Territory of Government. *Economy and Society,* 25: 3, 327–46.

Simon, J. (2007) *Governing Through Crime: How the War on Crime Transformed American Democracy and Created a Culture of Terror.* New York, Oxford University Press.

Social Exclusion Unit (1998) *Bringing Britain Together: A National Strategy for Neighbourhood Renewal: The Report of Policy Action Team 12 – Young People.* London, Stationary Office.

Taylor-Gooby, P. (2003) *The Genuinely Liberal Genuine Welfare State.* Paper presented at the Social Policy Association Conference, University of Teeside, 16 July.

Willis, P. (1997) *Learning to Labour: How Working Class Kids Get Working Class Jobs.* London, Saxon House.

Young, J. (1999) *The Exclusive Society.* London, Sage.

Youth Justice Board (2005) *Annual Statistics 2003/4.* London, Youth Justice Board.

CHAPTER 2

Legal Literacy in Practice With Children and Families

Michael Preston-Shoot

Introduction

Practitioners not uncommonly express anxiety about social work's relationship with law. They may be concerned about how it strikes a balance between care and control, needs and resources, or risk and autonomy. They may be critical of the dominance of some social divisions in framing legal rules, which affect people's well being, or of the over-representation of other groups in coerced interventions. They may worry about scrutiny of their practice by legal practitioners or fear that social work's values and purposes will become distorted by statutory powers and duties. However, whilst some legal rules do exert control over individuals defined as a risk or at risk, others allocate resources to meeting need, promote equality and offer protection from harm. Either way, law is one source of a social worker's power.

Practitioners may also feel ill-at-ease with exercising authority and control (Beckett, 2009; Braye and Preston-Shoot, 2009). They may be concerned about how service users will perceive legally mandated interventions, such as court directed assessments (*Children Act 1989*) enforced contact arrangements (*Children and Adoption Act 2006*) approved child protection measures (*Children Act 1989*) or endorsed recommendations to curtail young people's offending (*Criminal Justice and Immigration Act 2008*). However, legal rules also bring transparency to the social worker-service user relationship (Campbell and Davidson, 2009). Thus, whilst social workers should not underestimate their positional power (Davies, 2009) derived from training, legislative authority, professional status, access to information and resources, organisational location and job role, neither should they exaggerate it. Whether in youth justice or childcare, court approval is necessary to exercise statutory authority that curtails liberty or seeks to safeguard and protect. Moreover, coercive powers are much less a feature of the legal framework than commonly assumed (Braye and Preston-Shoot, 2009). Checks and balances surround the social work role, derived for instance from parental responsibility, child and family involvement in decision-making, and the impact of human rights and administrative law.

Practitioners may also be concerned about the impact of organisational policies and practices on social work and on service users. They may point to service user criticisms of how agencies have neglected their experiences and needs (Campbell and Davidson, 2009; Preston-Shoot, 2010a). Most social workers are conscientious (Re F [2008]) and perform valuable work that demonstrates dedication, skill and care in meeting people's complex needs (Re X (Emergency Protection Orders) [2006]; Re B [2007]; Re D [2008]). Of concern, however, is judicial recognition that they are also overworked and lacking the resources to uphold the highest practice standards (Re F [2008]). Indeed, the impact of being inundated with service demands has a long history, as does Ombudsman concern about incidents of neglect and mistreatment of service users and judicial criticism of unlawful interpretation of legal rules (Braye and Preston-Shoot, 2009).

Law has been a prescribed component of qualifying social work education since child protection inquiries (Blom-Cooper, 1985) and research (Ball et al., 1988) highlighted the extent of practitioner uncertainty about, and ignorance of the legal rules for practice. Increasingly, law teaching on social work programmes has been positively evaluated but social workers continue to express lack of confidence in their knowledge and competence for working in the legal arena (Braye and Preston-Shoot, 2009). Moreover, mental health inquiries and investigation into serious case reviews similarly reveal practitioner and manager ignorance and uncertainty concerning the legal rules (Sheppard, 1996; Ofsted, 2009).

Indeed, understanding of and compliance with statutory requirements is currently under the policy spotlight. Laming (2009a) in his progress report, comments that professionals must understand the legal framework. He argues that the legal rules are not well understood, highlighting here those relating to information sharing and inter-agency collaboration. He encourages social workers to be confident and decisive in using legal options. Moreover, he demands robust and consistent implementation of policies, procedures and legislation. In his subsequent evidence to a House of Commons select committee (Laming, 2009b) he argues that front-line staff are not well equipped in relation to the legislation, policy guidance and practice guidance that underpins their practice.

Ofsted (2009) in an overview of serious case reviews, has also noted instances where legal rules have not been followed when assessing children's needs and placing them with foster carers. However, in its analysis the inspectorate does not interrogate whether its findings are the outcome of social worker uncertainty about the legal rules and/or the elevation by their employing authorities of in-house procedures that may not necessarily be an accurate interpretation of the law. The process of translation of the law-in-theory to the law-in-practice remains unacknowledged and beyond scrutiny. Equally, Laming in his analysis

(2009a) appears to conflate the legislative base with local authority procedures and fails also to interrogate this process of translation. He neither scrutinises how power is exercised in bureaucratic organisations or how social workers experience the exercise by managers of positional authority in which organisational decision-making may run counter to how social workers understand the legal rules and the values and knowledge bases informing their assessments, investigations and recommendations.

The purpose of this chapter, then, is to offer some critical reflections when outlining the legal dimensions of social work with children and their families, and exploring the nature and extent of their powers. A critical lens will also be cast on the organisational context of social work practice and on the interface between law and ethics, analysing various dualities such as care and control, needs and resources, and professional autonomy versus employer direction, that reside within social work roles and tasks.

Body of the legal rules

Practitioners and students have reported that the law is often implicit in agency practice, which is shaped by organisational procedures (Braye et al., 2007). The Social Work Task Force (2009) has recognised that understanding of legislation is essential for quality social work practice. The House of Commons Select Committee (2009) has observed, however, that councils are struggling to meet their statutory commitments.

In fact, one starting point for practice should be the body of the legal rules, the basic skeleton for which is provided by primary legislation (Acts of Parliament). Acts are then fleshed out by secondary legislation (Regulations within Statutory Instruments) and by policy guidance and practice guidance issued by central government departments. Policy guidance, sometimes referred to as statutory guidance, is issued under section 7, Local Authority Social Services Act 1970, and must be followed (R (AB and SB) v Nottingham CC [2001]). Even practice guidance, whilst advisory, should not be departed from without good reason since it outlines the shape of good social work practice (R v Islington LBC, ex parte Rixon [1996]). Judges may also have to rule on the interpretation and extent of particular legal rules, such as the meaning of the likelihood of significant harm (Re H and R (Child Sexual Abuse: Standard of Proof) [1996]), when children may be removed from families at the interim order stage in care proceedings (Re L-A (Children) [2009]), or the process to be followed by a local authority when applying for an emergency protection order (X Council v B (Emergency Protection Orders [2004]; Re X (Emergency Protection Orders [2006]). These examples illustrate that case law must also form part of social workers' necessary legal literacy.

If this is the law-in-theory, a process of translation then takes place within social work organisations (Preston-Shoot, 2010a). This law-in-between turns the legal rules into agency procedures. That process of translation should be scrutinised by inspectorates and employees alike to ensure that interpretation of the legal rules is defensible. Equally, the law-in-practice should also be monitored to ensure that the decisions that practitioners and managers take are also lawful. This is because some local authorities have sought to avoid their legal duties, for instance towards asylum seeking minors under the *Children Act 1989* and the *Children (Leaving Care) Act 2000* (R (Behre and Others) v Hillingdon LBC [2003]; R (S) v Sutton LBC [2007]). Judicial reviews have also quashed flawed assessments and service provision, for example care plans for disabled children where needs have not been properly assessed (R (LH and MH) v Lambeth LBC [2006]).

Primary and secondary legislation mainly delegates powers and duties to councils with social services responsibilities. Social workers and their employing organisations must, therefore, act within the legal rules. This is the source of their lawful authority. Thus, practice in R (G) v Nottingham CC [2008] drew heavy judicial criticism because a child was removed from parents without lawful authority. Similarly, in a case involving a disabled young woman and her family, because a local authority's decision-making met none of the requirements within the *Children Act 1989* in respect of minimising the effects of disability and ascertaining and paying due regard to the wishes and feelings of those involved (R (CD and VD) v Isle of Anglesey CC [2004]).

Additionally, there are also legal rules that govern how lawful authority should be exercised. Known as administrative law, case law over the years has codified principles for the exercise of power, namely that practice should demonstrate:

* Meaningful consultation prior to decisions.
* Sharing of information on which reliance is placed.
* That decisions are reasonable by reference to values and knowledge, applied with skill through assessment to an individual case.
* Clear reasons for decisions, preferably given in writing.
* Opportunities for people affected by the exercise of authority to challenge decisions.
* How European convention rights have been promoted.
* How duties under equality legislation have been considered.
* Procedural fairness.

Essentially standards for decision-making and the conduct of interventions, these principles set a benchmark not just for how authority is actually used. Legislation provides social workers with powers, or permissions to act, and with duties, or directions to act. Both normally require the exercise of discretion, meaning a process of decision-making to conclude whether particular circumstances indicate that duties and/or powers must be implemented. It should be possible, therefore, to see how these standards have framed the decision whether or not to act. Once again, case law and Ombudsman reports illustrate how these standards are sometimes departed from, for instance in the handling of complaints, statements by young people that they are being abused or neglected by foster parents, and partnership in care proceedings (Braye and Preston-Shoot, 2009). When the Social Work Task Force (2009) refers approvingly to practitioners keeping service users involved and taking care to ensure that they understand a situation, administrative law principles provide a legal underpinning for such statements about good practice.

The body of the legal rules also requires positive action from public bodies, including local authorities. One such collection of requirements, when exercising statutory authority, resides in equality legislation. Currently[0] the Race Relations (Amendment) Act 2000, the *Disability Discrimination Act 2005* and the *Equality Act 2006* require public bodies to counteract discrimination and promote equal opportunities when providing goods and services. Practice, however, appears somewhat variable. Judicial reviews have found that local authorities have used eligibility criteria to deny disabled children and their families assessments and services, breaching both *Children Act 1989* duties to minimise the effect of disability and to ascertain and consider their wishes and feelings, and *Disability Discrimination Act 2005* duties to pay due regard to an equality impact assessment (R (CD and VD) v Isle of Anglesey CC [2004]; R (JL) v Islington LBC [2009]). In cutting the financial support given to voluntary organisations, not all local authorities have conducted or paid due regard to the findings of race or disability equality impact assessments (R (Chavda) v Harrow LBC [2008]; R (Meany and Others) v Harlow DC [2009]; R (Kaur and Shah) v Ealing LBC [2008]). Inspections have also reported much activity around equality and diversity but have recommended the review of policies on assessment and care planning, the further development of culturally appropriate provision, and the need for positive leadership (CSCI, 2008a; b; 2009).

Another collection of requirements resides in the *Human Rights Act 1998*, which integrated the European Convention on Human Rights into United Kingdom law. Public bodies must positively promote Convention rights and act proportionately when qualifying them. The *Human Rights Act 1998*, in line with Article 6 of the Convention, the right to a fair trial, and Article 13, the right to an effective remedy, has strengthened procedural rights and opened up local authorities to challenges in respect of how they have exercised statutory power. In children's services successful claims have included cases where personal injury has followed negligent failure to properly discharge child protection duties (Barrett v Enfield LBC [1999]; NXS v Camden LBC [2009]) or to act in good faith when providing information on which others will rely (W and Others v Essex CC and Another [2000]).

The balance of power in children's services has also been recalibrated. The *Children Act*

---

[0] The Equality Bill current being debated in Parliament may amend this framework.

1989 gave courts the power to direct local authorities to conduct assessments (section 38 [6]) and to impose any order in family proceedings. Courts must also support applications for child assessment, emergency protection and care orders, or for restriction or termination of contact. The exercise of statutory authority in social work practice has subsequently also been opened up for scrutiny by the introduction of independent reviewing officers to monitor how local authorities implement care plans for looked after young people (*Adoption and Children Act 2002*), of advocacy for children who wish to make representations and complaints (*Adoption and Children Act 2002*), access to information (*Data Protection Act 1998*). However, research has found that young people and their families may experience difficulty in deriving full benefit from these new process and already existing complaints procedures (Braye and Preston-Shoot, 2009).

Finally, legal rules also govern when local authorities may (not) take their resources into account. In essence, they may take resources into account when setting eligibility criteria but not when assessing need. If, following assessment, an authority determines that it should further intervene, resources may be taken into account when deciding on a care plan but intervention must have a reasonable chance of meeting the needs identified (Braye and Preston-Shoot, 2009). Decisions that are resource-led and will not meet assessed needs, for instance of young people leaving care (R (M) v Hammersmith and Fulham LBC [2008]) or of special guardians and foster parents (B v Lewisham LBC and Others [2008]), are unlawful. The Social Work Task Force (2009) has recognised too that weaknesses in resources have meant that people have not received high quality services. However, in recommending that sufficient resources are provided so that social workers can do their job well, the Task Force has been less than stridently critical in the face of evidence which points to the quality of services, for instance for looked after children or the commencement of care proceedings, being affected by a culture of budget-led rather than needs-led decision-making. Equally worrying has been the initial government response (Burnham and Balls, 2009), to the effect that actions must be affordable and local authorities will have to find more efficient means of organising teams and supporting practitioners.

Although the body of the legal rules sets out responsibilities for how social work should be conducted, and powers and duties for how the needs of children and their families should be met, law alone is an insufficient map (Braye and Preston-Shoot, 2006). The discretion contained within powers and duties, for example in the *Children Act 1989*, means that statutory authority may be exercised restrictively or expansively, and the case law quoted herein illustrates the impact that resource levels and attitudes can have on decision-making. Moreover, law does not provide a clear map for practice. The interface between childcare and young offender legislation provides one such illustration in relation to the paramountcy of the child's welfare. Another is found in the oscillation in the legal rules between paternalism, autonomy and empowerment in respect of children, and between meeting accusations of doing too much too soon or too little too late. Finally, even if helpful as a map, practitioners may not arrive at the supposed destination because of emotional dynamics surrounding a case or the pressures that arise when working alongside other professionals. Hence, social workers should critically appraise the legal mandate, drawing on their practice wisdom, research knowledge, values and service user feedback. Case-making skills will depend not just on how legal knowledge and understanding is used.

Code of practice

To practise as social workers, practitioners must be registered with a care council (*Care Standards Act 2000*). As part of their registration, they are required to uphold a code of practice (GSCC, 2002). Amongst other requirements, they must promote the rights of service users and carers and act lawfully. Their legal powers and duties are, therefore, centre stage amongst their obligations as social workers. Equally, legal rules are also implicit amongst other practice obligations. Registered social workers must emphasise human dignity and worth, a clear reference to human rights within the European Convention on Human Rights integrated into UK law by the *Human Rights Act 1998*. They must enhance people's well-being and ensure their protection which, in the context of practice with children and their families, directs social workers to, amongst other legal rules, the *Children Act 1989*, *Children Act 2004*, and the *Adoption and Children Act 2002*. They must also challenge and work to improve agency policies, procedures and service provision, and notify employers of resource or other difficulties that impact on safe working. These requirements mean that social workers must be aware of their obligations under the code of practice, including where necessary drawing on the *Public Interest Disclosure Act 1998*.

Employers also have obligations under the code of practice. They must give staff information about relevant legislation for their work. The legal rules are once again explicitly highlighted. However, as for practising social workers, they are similarly implicit in other obligations facing their managers who must establish systems to facilitate reporting of operational difficulties (*Public Interest Disclosure Act 1998*), support social workers so as not to put their registration at risk, provide effective supervision and ensure commitment to social work values and knowledge. These requirements engage employment law and the relationship of trust which must exist between employers and employees.

As yet the employers' section of the code does not have statutory force, with the result that it is difficult for employees and regulators to hold organisations delivering social work services directly accountable for their practice with respect to their codified responsibilities. Proposals have been made to rectify this gap in the regulatory mosaic (House of Commons

2009; Laming, 2009a) but legislation will be required. An interim measure would be for Ofsted and the Care Quality Commission, in their inspection functions, to include an evaluation of how agencies respond to their codified obligations but this would require a greater engagement with front-line staff than either inspectorate has demonstrated hitherto.

Similarly, it is questionable how far the code of practice has impacted on social workers' behaviour and on their perception of the employer-employee relationship. Although adherence to the code is required for their continued licence to practise, and is therefore their ultimate accountability (Kline, 2009), the evidence suggests that social workers are hesitant about challenging their employers. It also reveals that social workers are either uncertain of the legal rules or knowingly complicit in organisational decision-making which fails to follow statutory guidance, accepts poor practice standards, unlawfully prioritises resources rather than people's needs, seeks to avoid legal duties and/or endorses flawed assessments and service provision (Preston-Shoot, 2010a). One option for embedding ethics more centrally in practice would be to make the code of practice an express term of each social worker's employment contract (Preston Shoot and Kline, 2009).

As it is, the accountability mosaic remains muddled in two crucial respects. The code assumes that the relationship between law and ethics, in theory and in practice, is unproblematic. It also fails to clarify the relationship between social workers' ethical principles and their employment contract. The Task Force (2009) in its final report, does not recommend making the employers' code of practice statutory. Nor does it recommend clarifying the code's status. Rather, to improve the organisational context within which social workers practise, it advises that employers guarantee standards for support and supervision, against which their performance can be assessed and action plans for improvement published. When exercising power and authority the interface between law and ethics and between practitioners and their organisational environment deserve critical attention

Social work values

When and how to intervene in situations may not be obvious by reference to the legal rules alone (Braye and Preston-Shoot, 2009). Equally, the exercise of power over others may only be justifiable, or indeed have the potential to be empowering, if framed within a set of values (Campbell and Davidson, 2009; Davies, 2009). Thus, social work has drawn on traditional and more radical values to underpin practice with attentiveness and responsiveness to need, integrity and fairness, and respect towards individuals whilst challenging oppression. Such values find some support both within child care legislation and also administrative law and the *Human Rights Act 1998*. Thus, a values literacy may be helpful in order to capture desired outcomes in a case, the extent of concepts such as confidentiality and partnership, and a way forward when different interests conflict (Preston-Shoot et al., 2001).

However, three challenges arise. The first is ethical erosion. Judges (for instance in R (L and Others) v Manchester CC [2002]; Re F [2008]) and research (Marsh and Triseliotis, 1996; Preston-Shoot, 2010a; Preston-Shoot et al., 2001) have criticised the erosion of values in agency policies and practice, and expressed concern about social workers' apparent loss of an ethical orientation in the face of organisational and managerial pressures. Equally, however, ethical erosion may be seen when law-making is affected by moral panics, as evidenced in respect of people seeking asylum and children who commit offences.

The second is muddle, complexity and lack of specificity within social work values. The charge here is that it remains unclear what might represent a breach of a value principle, or component of an ethical code, and that statements of values are richly evocative but much thinner in how they might actually inform practice (Braye and Preston-Shoot, 2009). As Dickson (2009) wryly observes, it could be possible to have conduct that is ethical or unethical depending on which standard is actually applied.

The third challenge is the relationship between law and ethics. Some practice may be lawful but unethical, as in an adoption case (Re F [2008]). Similarly, some practice may be ethical but unlawful, for instance when attempting to meet the needs of failed asylum seekers. Besides maintaining a critical watchfulness on the values that the legal rules express, social workers also have to think through their response when law and ethics collide in specific cases.

The organisational domain

Ideally the organisational environment in which social workers practise would be empowering, supportive and competent. Continuing professional development would be valued as enabling practitioners to maintain their knowledge base and contribute to a learning environment. Workloads would be managed to reflect each practitioner's experience and expertise, and to promote a quality service. Supervision would enable constructive challenge and reflective scrutiny of the work, including how such conflicting imperatives as care and control might be balanced, how inter-agency dynamics and relationships with and between family members impact on decision-making, and how legal powers and duties might assist in safeguarding and promoting the welfare of children and their families. Power would be explicitly interrogated in all interactions between practitioners and managers and between agency staff and service users.

However, the development and maintenance of legal competence has been a neglected aspect of continuing professional development, other than for Approved Mental Health

Professionals and for some workers studying for post-qualifying child care awards. Yet legal literacy is crucial in enabling practitioners to respond authoritatively and coherently when organisational realities, such as resource constraints, impact on decision-making. Moreover, continuing professional development has not been properly valued by employers (Social Work Task Force, 2009) and vacancy levels and workload pressures restrict the capacity to resource it (House of Commons, 2009). Escalating demand and resource pressures have also meant that workloads have been unrealistic and impacted negatively on staff development and quality practice (Social Work Task Force, 2009). Such pressures have led the select committee (House of Commons, 2009) to be sceptical about the ability of employers to resource developmental programmes for newly qualified social workers.

Research, including meta-analyses of serious case reviews and child protection inquiries, indicates that these realities of front line practice are longstanding, as is the neglect of how aspiring and newly qualified practitioners experience situations where they could have made the best decisions possible but are castigated for not securing the ideal outcome (Marsh and Triseliotis, 1996; Braye and Preston-Shoot, 2009; Preston-Shoot, 2010b). Moreover, some appeals by social workers against deregistration have been successful because, whatever the shortcomings in their work, their practice has been negatively affected by lack of support and inadequate supervision, allocation of excessive responsibility and work beyond their level of professional development, and chaotic organisational environments (LA v GSCC [2007]; Forbes v GSCC [2008]; Cordingley v Care Council for Wales [2009]).

The organisational domain may, therefore, be a setting where practitioners and managers (un)knowingly depart from best practice and fail to challenge unlawful and/or unethical practice. In such a context, practitioners' learning about law and ethics may appear less relevant than the organisation's own procedures when, in fact, it should act as a counterpoint to the influence of agency culture on perceptions of roles and tasks (Horwath, 2007; Preston-Shoot, 2010b). Noteworthy here is that, whilst the Task Force (2009) and Laming (2009a) are critical of aspects of the working environment for social workers, and urge that they be provided with the resources and conditions needed to practise effectively, they omit to analyse why organisational shortcomings are so persistent and what their impact is on the recognition and meeting of people's needs. Nor do they comment on organisational hostility towards whistle blowers or challenge how service provision has become adjusted to (distorted by) targets, inadequate funding, excessive workloads, restrictive provision and organisational procedures, in so doing undermining legal rules, service user needs, quality practice based on skilled use of knowledge about child and family development, and compliance with the GSCC code (2002).

Nowhere do they critique how agencies can become enclosed organisations where conformity to procedures and culture is elevated above independent thought and judgement, or reflect on the dangers when the employment relationship becomes more powerful than external professional accountability (Preston-Shoot, 2010a; Preston-Shoot and Kline, 2009). Nowhere do they respond to research (Braye et al., 2007) that has found the role of organisations to be crucial in creating or sustaining a learning environment in which law, ethics and research informed knowledge can be seen as an explicit and significant feature of practice. In short they appear at best muted and at worst silent on how narrow definitions of need become institutionalised and lodged firmly in organisational arrangements, relegating to the sidelines people's perspectives, priorities and narratives, and how social work has institutionalised a bureaucratic, procedural frame of reference that does not encourage use of practitioner knowledge, including thinking about legal rules, reflection about values, and appraisal about the use of different sources of power.

Using power

When deciding to use statutory powers or to exercise discretionary duties practitioners will be influenced by their orientations to practice. These same orientations will shape their response to questions of balancing legal rules against professional values and knowledge, and weighing rights and autonomy against protection from risk. They may prioritise doing things right, drawing upon a technical knowledge and interpretation of particular legal rules. Alternatively, they may emphasise doing right things, where the motivating force is less whether a legal rule may be applied to a specific situation than an underpinning value or ethical principle. However, they may foreground right thinking, where the impetus for acting is a notion of human rights (Braye and Preston-Shoot, 2006; 2009). In many cases, practitioners may draw on more than one of these orientations as a justification for action.

An alternative conceptualisation (Braye and Preston-Shoot, 2007; 2009) is to distinguish between:

- A technical orientation to practice, which highlights accurate legal knowledge.
- A needs-led approach, which foregrounds people's experience and the obligations owed to vulnerable individuals and families.
- A procedural frame of reference, which prioritises an employer's policies and expectations for implementing the legal rules.
- A rights-based perspective, which draws on how legal rules confer and limit human rights, and which seeks to promote the rights people hold.

These orientations are not automatically right or wrong – each merely brings a different contribution to the task of practising soundly within the legal framework. If practitioners already have a rounded profile in terms of their orientations, then all well and good. If they routinely rank one more highly, then it will be worth considering how to achieve a better balance in their practice.

Within both of these approaches to conceptualising the impetus behind decision-making one may question whether practice is essentially reformist, working within official rules and structures where power resides with professionals, or anti-oppressive in the sense of exploring the political context explicitly and offering a partnership within which there is not just a transfer of power through involvement but a conscious decision to enable service users to find their own sources of power, including through the legal rules such as those relating to advocacy, complaints, equality, partnership and rights.

Rees (1991) describes practice as illustrating one, two or three dimensional power relationships. In one-dimensional relationships practitioners control the agenda and demand compliance with their rules. Two-dimensional relationships are reformist in the sense of enabling service users to participate in shaping the boundaries and content of the work. Three dimensional relationships offer an anti-oppressive approach to practice, which engages with how legal rules present images of people, aims to promote rights, and offers workers' knowledge and skills to enable service users to achieve individual and social change. This level of analysis recognises that legal rules can be a force for or a barrier to change. They may be used to capture people's interests, needs, responsibilities and relationships. Alternatively, more empowering interpretations of particular legal rules may be possible, for instance where children's rights are aligned with notions of need and care. Anti-oppressive practice will seek to maximise people's control over defining their interests and needs and to challenge how images of relationships have been defined. Power is discussed openly – when and how statutory or positional authority might be used, how agency decision-making is constructed, what power service users have and how practitioners conceive partnership working.

Sometimes people will have no choice but to work with social workers, as in child protection investigations or following sentencing in the youth court. Sometimes they may request that social workers use their statutory powers, for instance when accommodating children (section 20, *Children Act 1989*). People in a relationship do not always have equal power and there will be occasions when social workers cannot deny, delegate or ignore statutory powers and duties (Braye and Preston-Shoot, 2009). However, they can still be held accountable through administrative law standards and mechanisms of redress (complaints procedures, judicial review, Ombudsman investigations) for the proportionality of their interventions (*Human Rights Act 1998*). They can demonstrate empowering skills as much when seeking to protect individuals from abuse and neglect (section 47, *Children Act 1989*; Article 3, ECHR), motivated by a duty of care, as when promoting autonomy and family life (section 17, *Children Act 1989*; Article 8 ECHR). These include promoting the exercise of power by service users, communicating clearly about when and why social work tasks might demand the use of powers and duties, building relationships that address the legacy of powerlessness and involve people in need analysis and problem definition, and exploring options for achieving desired goals. As service users consistently point out, if practitioners are motivated by principles of avoiding harm and seeking benefit, if they are treated justly and with respect, and involved, then relationships and interventions, even when imposed or coerced, are more likely to be experienced positively, (Campbell and Davidson, 2009; Davies, 2009; Preston-Shoot, 2010a).

Conclusion

This chapter has argued that legal, ethical and organisational literacy are essential underpinnings for a considered, proportional and empowering use of power and authority. Gaps in legal knowledge will disadvantage practitioners, and the service users they are working with, in negotiations within their own agency and with other professionals. Gaps between espoused and practised values will generate cynicism and potentially have harmful effects for service users. The chapter has also implied that emotional, professional resilience will be necessary to comment, challenge, critique and reassess how organisations exercise the statutory mandates bequeathed by Parliament to them. Quality practice will be the skilled application of a distillation of knowledge and understanding, unique in every case that enables practitioners to connect the relevant legal rules with professional priorities and the objectives of ethical practice.

Individual practitioners must take responsibility for their own practice. This includes questioning how they have become socialised into their profession, given the impact of organisational hierarchy, location and funding on practice standards, evaluation of staff performance and the framing of tasks. They must bring together legal and ethical knowledge, and determine the extent of each in every case. They must manage situations when legal rules might create ethical problems and when ethical principles might fall foul of statutory duties. They must manage situations when local authorities act unlawfully or fail to meet ethical standards, demonstrating a professional, moral responsibility to scrutinise organisational (in)action and to challenge poor practice. It is a daunting prospect but standards for the exercise of power and authority require no less.

References

Ball, C., Harris, R., Roberts, G. and Vernon, S. (1988) *The Law Report. Teaching and Assessment of Law in Social Work Education*. London: CCETSW.

Beckett, C. (2009) The ethics of control. *Ethics and Social Welfare*, 3: 3, 229–33.

Blom-Cooper, L. (1985) *A Child in Trust. The Report of the Panel of Inquiry into the Circumstances Surrounding the Death of Jasmine Beckford*. London Borough of Brent.

Braye, S. and Preston-Shoot, M. (2006) The role of law in welfare reform: critical perspectives on the relationship between law and social work practice. *International Journal of Social Welfare*, 15: 1, 19–26.

Braye, S. and Preston-Shoot, M. (2007) *All in day's work*. London: Social Care Institute for Excellence. Reusable electronic learning object, available at: http://www.scie.org.uk/publications/elearning/index.asp and at: http://www.jorum.ac.uk

Braye, S. and Preston-Shoot, M. (2009) *Practising Social Work Law*. 3rd edn. Basingstoke: Palgrave Macmillan.

Braye, S., Preston-Shoot, M. and Thorpe, A. (2007) Beyond the Classroom: Learning Social Work Law in Practice. *Journal of Social Work*, 7: 3, 322–40.

Burnham, A. and Balls, E. (2009) *Government Response to the Social Work Taskforce*. London: HMSO.

Campbell, J. and Davidson, G. (2009) Coercion in the Community: A Situated Approach to The Examination of Ethical Challenges For Mental Health Social Workers. *Ethics and Social Welfare*, 3: 3, 249–63.

CSCI (2008a) *Putting People First: Equality and Diversity Matters 1. Providing Appropriate Services for Lesbian, Gay and Bisexual and Transgender People*. London: Commission for Social Care Inspection.

CSCI (2008b) *Putting People First: Equality and Diversity Matters 2. Providing Appropriate Services for Black and Minority Ethnic People*. London: Commission for Social Care Inspection.

CSCI (2009) *Putting People First: Equality and Diversity Matters. Achieving Disability Equality in Social Care Services*. London: Commission for Social Care Inspection.

Davies, H. (2009) Ethics and Practice in Child Protection. *Ethics and Social Welfare*, 3: 3, 322–8.

Dickson, D. (2009) When Law and Ethics Collide: Social Control in Child Protective Services. *Ethics and Social Welfare*, 3: 3, 264–83.

GSCC (2002) *Codes of Practice for Social Care Workers and Employers*. London: General Social Care Council.

Horwath, J. (2007) The Missing Assessment Domain: Personal, Professional and Organisational Factors Influencing Professional Judgements When Identifying and Referring Child Neglect. *British Journal of Social Work*, 37: 8, 1285–303.

House of Commons Children, Schools and Families Committee (2009) *Training of Children and Families Social Workers. Seventh Report of Session 2008–09*. London: The Stationery Office.

Kline, R. (2009) *What If? Social Care Professionals and the Duty of Care. A Practical Guide to Staff Duties and Rights*. Wakefield: Association of Professionals in Education and Children's Trusts.

Laming, H. (2009a) *The Protection of Children in England: A Progress Report*. London: HMSO.

Laming, H. (2009b) *The Protection of Children in England: Lord Laming's Progress Report*. Evidence to the Children, Schools and Families Committee, House of Commons. London: The United Kingdom Parliament.

Marsh, P. and Triseliotis, J. (1996) *Ready to Practise? Social Workers and Probation Officers: Their Training and First Year in Work*. Aldershot: Avebury.

Ofsted (2009) *Learning Lessons from Serious Case Reviews: Year 2*. Manchester: Ofsted.

Preston-Shoot, M. (2010a) On the Evidence For Viruses in Social Work Systems: Law, Ethics and Practice. *European Journal of Social Work*, (in press).

Preston-Shoot, M. (2010b) 'Looking After Social Work Practice in its Organisational Context: Neglected and Disconcerting Questions. In Ayre, P. and Preston-Shoot, M. (Eds.) *Children's Services at the Crossroads: A Critical Evaluation of Contemporary Policy for Practice*. Lyme Regis: Russell House Publishing.

Preston-Shoot, M. and Kline, R. (2009) Memorandum of Written Evidence. In House of Commons Children, Schools and Families Committee *Training of Children and Families Social Workers. Seventh Report of Session 2008–09*. Volume II. London: HMSO.

Preston-Shoot, M., Roberts, G. and Vernon, S. (2001) Values in Social Work Law: Strained Relations or Sustaining Relationships? *Journal of Social Welfare and Family Law*, 23: 1, 1–22.

Rees, S. (1991) *Achieving Power. Practice and Policy in Social Welfare*. North Sydney: Allen and Unwin.

Sheppard, D. (1996) *Learning the Lessons*. 2nd edn. London: Zito Trust.

Social Work Task Force (2009) *Building a Safe, Confident Future*. London: Department for Children, Schools and Families.

CHAPTER 3

Ethics and Power: A Discourse

Tom Wilks

Introduction

It is one of the ironies of social work practice that the world outside of social work perceives social workers as powerful agents of the state whereas social workers themselves, describing their work, can sometimes lack a sense of power and agency in their day to-day practice. Witness the contrast between on the one hand the *Daily Mail* headline 'Social workers snatch baby from mother 'not clever enough to raise a child' after she flees to Ireland to give birth' (Smith Squire, 2010) with on the other Jones description, based on interviews with practitioners, of social work as a 'traumatised occupation which has lost any sense of itself' (Jones, 2001: 550). This is one of a number of reasons why any discussion of the ethics of power in social work is so complex, yet so central to social work. Debates around the dual functions of care and control, of welfare versus protection in work with children and families, have been with us since the profession's inception and early development (Russel Day, 1981; Jones, 1983). However the current context of practice, the pressures under which practitioners work and the organisational contexts in which they operate, demands that we look at this issue afresh (Garret, 2009; Ayre and Preston Shoot, 2010). One important way of doing this is to look at power as an ethical practice issue and to explore the possibilities the expanding corpus of work on social work ethics offers us for insights into an area which has always sat at the heart of practice. My intention in this chapter is to begin with a critique of the application of traditional ethical frameworks to power, then a discussion of how power impinges on practice with children and families. Finally the chapter explores two key ethical frameworks discourse ethics and the ethics of care and their applicability to questions of how power operates in professional practice.

A useful starting point for our exploration of the ethics of power in social work is to look at how an essentially principlist ethical framework can be applied to the sorts of complex and difficult decisions faced by social workers working with children. Principlism is the ethical approach with which we are most familiar in social work. Beauchamp and Childress' (1994) work is a prime example of the application of this approach to professional ethics. Acting ethically involves the interplay between principle and practice, with the careful scrutiny of a practice issue through the glass of principle leading us towards ethical practice. The use of Utilitarian or Kantian principles, a prevalent, ethical framework in social work, would also be an example of this type of approach.

Sarah Banks (2006) provides an excellent case example which illustrates this way of going about ethical decision-making. She provides a practice example of an ethical dilemma which will be familiar to anyone who has ever practiced social work, where the balance between risk to a child and the rights of a parent are considered. Banks' example revolves around decision-making for a mother convicted of infanticide in the past and now pregnant again. The model of ethical practice presented here is the balance model. In order to behave ethically here we need to weigh the risk to the child and the rights of a parent. A balance needs to be struck between on the one hand promoting the mother's capacity to be self-determining' and on the other the risk of harm to others, between 'Kantian principles' and 'utilitarian considerations'

How does this balance model work? One of the model's strength is that it offers a fairly systematic way of addressing practice dilemmas. We begin by looking at the technical aspect of decision-making. To make an ethically sound decision in this situation we need the best information we can get on outcome grounded in research. We then look at the sort of ethical considerations which might impact upon our decision. The decision making process involves the interplay between these principles and the case itself and it is in the to and fro between case and principle that the moral decision is made.

This essentially principlist account of care and control dilemmas is premised on the idea of social workers being autonomous powerful moral agents able to make effective ethical decisions in response to these types of dilemmas. There are three ways in which this model could be seen as problematic and I am going to explore each in turn. Firstly I want to argue that in adopting this approach we run the risk of ethical judgements collapsing into technical ones. Secondly this perspective is underpinned by a particular understanding of the professional practice world of social workers; it has as its premise the view that social workers are powerful autonomous sovereign professionals able to make decisions themselves. Finally the approach underplays the complexity of power in social work practice.

Nature of power in social work

I want to start by a consideration of the collapse of the ethical into the technical. For the social worker operating within a principlist 'balance' model, making an accurate assessment of risk is crucial and prefaces ethical judgements about the right outcome. Underlying practice here is an expectation that social workers can achieve an almost actuarial accuracy in predicting future outcomes in complex social situations (Banks, 2006). However as Carson and Bain (2008) point out when assessing risk 'there will always be incomplete information; that is the central characteristic of risk' (Carson and Bain, 2008: 153). So one of the paradoxes of risk assessment is that if we can predict outcome then risk no longer becomes an issue. If we believe otherwise we are probably falling prey to the common conflation of risk with dangerousness (Parton and Small, 1989). Linked to this issue is the fact that as McBeath and Webb (2002) suggest, social workers operate in bureaucratic organisations, dominated by standardised procedure, where their capacity to make independent professional judgements is limited. This managerial tendency is most marked in children's services (Parton, 1998).

My final point is about the nature of power within social work. Power for social work is not an unproblematic or easily defined concept. In many ways the archetype of social work power is the use of the coercive powers of the law to remove children at direct risk of harm. We can easily envisage circumstances where a social worker might in all probability have an ethical obligation to use such powers. If we imagine a mother admitted with injuries to an Accident and Emergency Department of a general hospital who discloses she has been the victim of domestic violence and that her children have also been subject to physical harm from her partner; the ethical decision to intervene here is a relatively straightforward one. For the professionals involved recourse to principles, (whether these are the Kantian principles of respecting autonomy or Utilitarian principles of maximising the benefit to all involved) offers a moral basis for action. Hugman (2005) discussing a similar scenario points out that in these circumstances the same decision would be made regardless of the moral framework chosen to inform it. In circumstances where we have predictability of outcome the use of principles is relatively straightforward.

This type of action by social workers is what Sheppard (2006: 106) would call 'overt coercion'. This is made up of two elements: firstly, the use of coercive power where force is imposed in some way to control others; secondly the use of legitimate power where the state, through law legitimates this action. When we think of child protection it is the use of this sort of power which springs most readily to mind.

Sheppard also describes a second form of professional power, 'latent coercion'. At its simplest this involves the damoclean threat of its overt sibling, which he argues hangs over much social work activity. I think however we can understand latent power as being more than just a product of the possibility of overt coercion. The power attendant upon social workers' professional expertise and role within a relationship with a service user or their control over resources through systematic processes of assessment, can also be categorised as latent coercion. One key element of that service user worker dyad is the impact of structural sources of power, which can marginalise service users leaving them disempowered. 'The space occupied by social work is defined by its position in the interface between the main stream and the marginal in society. It can be no surprise therefore that social work involves those that are poorest most disadvantaged and marginalised' (Sheppard, 2006: 40). The intersecting variables of social class, race, ethnicity, gender, disability and culture all impact upon the service user social worker relationship, (Thompson, 1993; Dominelli, 2002a).

The notion of professional knowledge and expertise leads us to a third form of professional power, which I want to call (borrowing from Foucault (Foucault, 1980)) immanent power (Juniper, 2008). Power here is not a possession of an individual social worker, or a function of a social role (Parsons, 1969) but the product of a set of social relations rather than subjective intentionality (Mills, 2003). This is rather akin to what Smith terms 'power as process' (Smith, 2008: 32). To understand how social work power operates here we think about Foucault's (sometimes overworked) equation between knowledge and power and social work as a social practice. Approached from this perspective we can see social work as increasingly characterised by the application of systematic and taxonomic field of knowledge to service users. The bureaucratic application of systematic mechanisms of assessment and the use of technical risk assessment tools are a part of this process (Howe, 1994).

I want to look at a case study at this point which I hope will serve the purpose (as a sort of thought experiment) of illustrating the problems inherent in this collapse of the ethical into the technical and the weaknesses of a principlist analysis. Moral philosophers have long used thought experiments as a way of exploring ethical ideas (Tittle, 2005). A classic example of this approach would be Rawls (1973) exploration of the Original position as a justification for his universalist liberal ethics, in relation to social justice. My own example is much more modest and simple than this in its scope.

I want to look at a case example. David is a 13 year old boy, who is the only child of his mother, Mary, a woman in her 40s. Mary has a long history of being admitted to psychiatric hospital and has been diagnosed as suffering from bi-polar disorder. When Mary is not well her behaviour is sometimes characterised by periods of profound depression when she is not able to do things for herself, does not eat and rarely gets out of bed. At other times Mary is sleepless and preoccupied by grandiose and somewhat unrealistic projects, often concerning business ideas which will make her fortune, and secure her and David's futures. Mary's mother, who lives nearby has always been a source of support for her daughter and her grandson. When Mary has not been around she has stepped in to care for David. However she is finding it increasingly difficult to give this help as she herself has been diagnosed with advanced breast cancer. For David's social worker this situation presents a practice dilemma. Should David remain with his mother or be placed elsewhere? Now this is a gross simplification of the options and choices facing practitioners in such circumstances.

And as we have already argued social workers,' decision-making is circumscribed by a raft of organisational constraints. Nonetheless looking at this situation can provide a catalyst for a broader consideration of the roles ethics might play here.

Say, like the ghost of Christmas future, I could take a social worker making this decision to two possible futures for David. In one future he has grown up with long-term supportive foster carers. He has prospered at school and later at university, and has found a good job, yet as an adult suffers from depression and mental health problems. He feels guilty about his estrangement from his mother and about her suicide. He finds it difficult to form relationships with other people and lacks a sense of self. In our second envisaged future David feels more positive about his relationship with his mother, recognises some of the good things that came from caring for her as an adolescent, things which he thinks have helped him be more caring in his current stable relationship. Although still sad, he was glad to have been around when she died from cancer. He does however regret the way in which his education has suffered and has always struggled to find work and this creates financial hardship and stress for him.

The problem for our time-travelling social worker here is that choosing between of these putative futures is virtually impossible. There are losses and gains in both scenarios, so even with 20/20 foresight, we are not able to solve our dilemma. This type of case and type of complex nuanced decision is commonplace in social work with children. Even if we have at our disposal a technology of risk assessment which enables us to predict what will happen to help us in a practice dilemma like this it does not necessarily enable us to make an ethically sound decision. So although we may desire a technical solution to our ethical dilemmas, often in real world situations recourse to such solutions will not help us and one of the reasons for this is that our decision has an important ethical dimension to it. This illustrates the weakness of social workers 'being construed as more akin to technicians or technical experts rather than reflective creative committed professionals' (Banks, 2004: 176) and ethics being 'mere social science' (Lovat and Gray, 2008: 1106).

Given that this is the case, can recourse to ethical principles help us decide the best course of action and a resolution to our dilemma. So let us move on here to look at how traditional ethics and recourse to principle might help resolve this dilemma. I think our thought experiment reveals some of the limitations of this approach. The utilitarian approach seems to offer us a possible framework for thinking about our envisaged futures. Applying a consequentialist approach when we know the consequences attendant on a given action seems an inherently attractive option here. However even if we only look at David here, (following our duty to make his welfare paramount) we meet difficulties. For whatever currency we use to measure these consequences happiness or good it is extremely difficult to judge one outcome against another. Here we come against an intrinsic problem with

35

utilitarianism the difficulty in 'showing that meaningful reckoning can be made of the advantages and disadvantages, in terms of the promotion of basic good, of different actions' (Clarke, 2000: 99).

Ethics, power and discourse

Over the past five years or so there has been increasing interest in and debate about the potential of an ethics based on discourse to offer an alternative to teleological and consequentialist approaches to values in social work. It has been around the issue of power in social work that much of this interest and debate has coalesced.

Houston outlines the basic tenet of Habermas's communicative approach to ethics as follows; 'communication and intersubjective engagement are the only media by which actors should reach morally binding decisions' (Houston, 2003: 822). Why has this approach proved so attractive to contemporary commentators on power in social work? I think there are two reasons for this; firstly its pragmatism which echoes many of the precepts of empowering practice in social care and secondly its democratically grounded claims to move beyond inter-subjectivism to provide a more universalistic ethics.

The first important point to make in this respect is that the application of Habermas's ethical thinking to social work is marked by a distinctly pragmatic focus (Habermas, 1984, 1987, 1990). We have already noted the gap that can exist between ethical principle and ethical decision-making grounded in practice. The focus of Habermas's work is on practical action, praxis, on the mechanisms we might employ to make morally appropriate decisions in circumstances marked by uncertainty and unpredictability. So for Habermas making the right decision is not about balancing competing principles, but about creating conditions which would allow an appropriate decision to be made. Social workers' professional existences are characterised by being confronted by a series of situations 'a complex amalgam of two individuals – social worker and client' (Lovat and Gray, 2008: 1109) where difficult ethical decisions have to be made. For proponents of a Habermasian view of ethics it is from a dialogue between service user and social worker that the ethical decision is generated. This potentially provides us with and ethics which is potentially 'particular and contextual' (Hugman, 2005: 127) and whose primary focus is inter-subjective and communicative.

Hayes and Houston (2007: 992) provide us with the most practice-focused account of this approach in relation to family group conferencing (FGC). Drawing our attention to the synergies that exist between a discursive ethical approach and the FGC model Hayes and Houston argue that the FGC (and other variants upon this overall approach) offer us a mechanism for negotiating outcomes to ethical practice dilemmas. Grounded in 'deliberative democracy' where 'recipients of social welfare are encouraged to become active agents constructing their needs interests and viewpoints' (Ibid.).

Hayes and Houston (2007: 990) argue that the FGC offers a space in which mediation can take place between 'life world ', a 'reservoir of shared, and often taken for granted, meanings which, through language shape our personalities and group identities' and 'system', the areas of life that are organised and controlled by the state' (more succinctly between family and state). What makes for an ethically sound process in this context? Hayes and Houston (2007: 1001–2) identify six elements which 'collectively summarise' Habermas's programme of discourse ethics and can be applied in this context, which I will briefly précis here. An ethical dialogue should be characterised by inclusivity with freedom for all participants to criticise and express themselves without restriction. Successful ethical dialogue should take place within an empathetic and respectful frame of reference. 'Power must be kept in check so that the only legitimate force is the force of better argument'. Finally reasoned argument rather than coercion should be the method adopted to seek consensus. This process enhances both the consensual power of the family and the power and capacity of the social workers working with them to address their problems.

One thing which immediately strikes us here is the way in which this perspective in its discussion of communication and dialogue echoes some of the precepts of empowering practice in social work (Adams, 2003) yet situates the concept ethically, thus creating a link with the elements of the social work value base which relate to social justice. We will explore this area further when we examine how this approach fits with the typography of power which was presented at the beginning of this chapter. However before we do this it is important to look at a second key element of this approach: its claims to universalism. One important issue which Banks (2006) raises in relation to inter-subjective and process focused approaches to ethics is that although they may enable us to engage more effectively with specific ethical issues within a localised sphere of practice, they are too local to act as the building blocks for a more ambitious project of constructing an ethics for a professional community. To do this we need to rely on some kind of approach more orientated to principle (whether the principles come from consequentialism, deontology or virtue ethics).

Habermasian discursive ethics are however ambitious in their scope and seek through their democratic focus orientation to establish a sort of claim for universality. It is this which I want to briefly explore now. Hugman (2005) argues that Habermas's ethics provide us with a bridge between our localised specific discussion of a particular set of circumstances to a more universal system of ethics through the idea of practical democratic discourse (the sort that might take place within a professional community such as social work). Hugman underlies the importance of Habermas's concept of democracy which underpins this aspect of his approach. A democratic society is characterised 'as one in which all people are able, as far as they have the capacity, to exchange ideas about truth, rightness and truthfulness' (Hugman, 2005: 129). Universality is derived from this democratic process. Within this democratic framework a morally valid decision is one in which the interests of all and perspectives of all are considered (Houston, 2003). So the principles which might obtain in respect of a Family Group Conference, making decisions about child protection and welfare, could also be applicable in respect of a broader community of common interest (the professional community of social work for example) providing universality at least in respect of the methods employed to obtain a valid moral decisions in practice.

I want to return the focus of our discussions at this point to the issue of power. As we have already seen this discursive approach to ethics offers two potentially attractive strands of thought. Firstly in its dialogic focus it has the potential to enable power to be shared between service users and social workers. Secondly it provides a universal system perhaps applicable in a wide variety of contexts.

Garrett (2009) argues that Habermasian ethics are underpinned by an overly simplistic account of power relations and as a consequence, 'Habermas's theorization does not provide social workers with an adequate basis for thought and praxis, because he fails to acknowledge how power differentials are apt to *complicate* (authors italics) even to undermine his discourse ethics and elaborate procedural framework' (Garrett, 2009: 873). It is possible to envisage how the discursive ethical practice outlined by Habermas might help us greatly when looking at decisions around the use of coercive power. However as we know power in social work is more complex than this and not easily simply reduced to a matter of overt coercion. The question the Habermasian position begs is about the viability of what Garret calls 'the utopia of perfectly transparent communication'. What I described earlier as latent power for example, is shaped by a web of interconnecting structural factors. If we acknowledge these must impinge upon the communicative process then this begins to undermine the process itself. If we then turn to the more Foucauldian conception of power I styled immanent power then it can be hard to see how a Habermasian approach can address this account of power relations marked by fluidity and omnipresence.

Feminist ethics and power

An exploration of how feminist approaches to social work practice and ethics might fit within the framework of Habermasian discourse ethics shows up underlines these weaknesses. 'Women have always been at the centre of the struggle to define the appropriate role for social work in rapidly changing societies' (Dominelli, 2002b: 17). Power and empowerment are vitally important themes in feminist approaches towards social work practice. The patriarchal oppression of women combines important coercive elements focused on male aggression and violence, an emphasis on the interpersonal and on relationships as a vehicle for the sustenance of male power, and the importance of ideology in underpinning the social construction of gender roles. A central tenet of feminist thought has always been the critical role played by the family in the sustenance and reproduction of social systems of power, 'the reproduction of everyday relations of domination' as Dominelli puts it (2002b: 68). The primary locus for the maintenance of patriarchal power has often been seen as the family and the coercive use of power within familial settings plays a central part in these processes (Dominelli, 2002; Mullender, 2002). For feminists the familial and the structural are symbiotically linked. When we consider the importance of social work with children and families in articulating the connection between the private and public spheres (life world and system), it is hard to conceive of a practice which does not take account of the insights of feminism. Drawing on Fraser's work (Fraser, 1989) Garret (2009) argues that Habermas's approach to the family occludes some of its potentially oppressive features. He argues that the approach in positing a situation where an idealised set of communicative relations exist ignores the fact that gender impinges on all our communication. Again power is more complex than we think.

What I have tried to do thus far is to explore some of the difficulties presented by applying a principlist framework to understanding the ethics of power in social work and then examine an alternative line of thinking, discursive ethics, developed from the work of Habermas, and explore its strengths and weaknesses as a framework for understanding power in social work with children and families. As we have seen feminist thinking has been the source of some of the most trenchant criticism of the Habermasian dialogic approach, whilst interestingly sharing its communicative focus. However it is when we come to consider the issue of power that the real differences between these approaches begin to emerge. Revisiting the notion/concept of autonomy serves to illuminate this further. We looked earlier at some of the problems for social work ethics presented by the notion of the autonomous social worker able to make independent rational decisions, as the actual experience of social workers working in child protection for local authorities undermines this way of thinking. Habermas's model of communicative ethics is also beset by some of these difficulties. For the transparent communication required by Habermasian discourse is premised on the notion of the participants in a dialogue not being undermined by the influence of power. As we have seen feminism with its emphasis on the influence of subliminal and coercive aspects of power on communication takes issue with this standpoint.

So how would feminist ethics help us to understand power? The foundations of the feminist ethic of care can be found in a critique of this concept of the autonomous (male) subject. The roots of this approach can be found in the debates between Kohlberg and Gilligan about the nature of moral reasoning (Gilligan, 1982; Kohlberg, 1981). Kohlberg conducted a series of psychological experiments with children looking at the types of cognitive processes they use to make ethical decisions. He found marked differences in his research between boys and girls. Boys he found were more likely to use abstract concepts when looking at ethical dilemmas and begin to apply universal moral principles and standards to particular cases. Girls contrastingly tended to respond to dilemmas in a much more pragmatic way, and explore the emotional parameters of the situations with which they were presented. Kohlberg argued that this difference was indicative of a staged process of moral development, in which the use of abstract concepts represented a higher level of reasoning than an engagement with the emotions of the participants in a dilemma. Boys he surmised were reaching this cognitive milestone more quickly than girls. However for Gilligan (who worked alongside Kohlberg on his investigations) these results could be interpreted in another way. She argued that what they demonstrated was a gender difference between the ways in which men and women address ethical issues, and that an ethics which is attentive to emotion and relationships is equally valid as a moral framework as one whose emphasis is on abstraction.

From this critical insight a complex ethical system sensitive to issues of power, an approach has developed which has been of increasing interest to social work (Larrabee, 1993; Bowden, 1997; Orme, 2002; Holland, 2009). What are the key features of the ethic of care and what sorts of insights can it provide when we come to consider questions about social work and power? As does discourse ethics, the ethics of care lays great emphasis on the centrality of our interactions with others and on communication generally in ethics. However where it differs is that, by emphasising care within relationships, it presents an account of that communicative process in which emotion and reciprocity are to the fore. What is key here is not just communication, but the nature of the relationship between the person cared for and the delivery of that care. That relationship is shaped by two things: firstly qualities to do with attendance to the needs of another (Tronto, 1993), attentiveness and reciprocity, which 'requires that we start from the standpoint of the one needing care – taking us a stage further than empathy' (Lloyd, 2006: 1178) secondly the grounding of the relationship itself in openness and honesty. The ethical professional is one who endeavours to build relationships which have these qualities. Feminist ethicists argue that patriarchal principle based approaches grounded in the notion of autonomy fail to grasp a basic fact about our interdependence upon one another, that 'the development of an autonomous adult human being requires nurture and care' (Lloyd, 2008).

Relationships are then fundamental to the feminist ethic of care. However to see this approach as simply as a counterpoint to principlism would be to ignore one further crucial aspect of this version account of ethics, its emphasis on caring as a practice. What makes this such an attractive way of thinking about professional ethics, is that care is so central to social work's professional project. In contrast to principlism the ethic of care is action orientated and concerned with the specific. 'In the framework of an ethics of care, the capacity to discern issues and to respond appropriately cannot be left to the workings of abstract principles but has to be teased out in the contexts of specific relationships' (Hugman, 2005: 71). To paraphrase Hugman, that means the relationship between *this* social worker and *this* service user. The ethic of care is action orientated and grounded in our lived professional experience, and places values firmly at the centre of everyday professional practice.

Use of power

I now want to think more specifically about the use of power, to consider how this model of ethics can help us in this area and think about what its weaknesses are. If we begin by thinking about latent power in social work the power attendant upon professional role and on difference we can begin to see how the feminist ethic of care might offer a potentially constructive approach with its emphasis on the relationship as the locus for ethical practice. Applying this ethical framework to social workers' relationships with service users would be characterised by two things. The first of these is honesty in respect of difference and its impacts on power. As ethical relationships are characterised by reciprocity, honesty is not just an expectation of the professional but of the service user as well, something the social worker will make explicit. Secondly an ethical relationship ought to be marked by attentiveness to the needs of service users grounded in an understanding of the emotional impacts of intervention and an empathetic understanding of their position. Being ethical would involve practising in a way which is consistent with the tenets.

As we have seen social work involves complex and nuanced decision making, particularly where the use of what we termed coercive powers is involved, the outcomes of which are often uncertain. Using traditional principle orientated approaches to ethics does not always enhance our capacity to make moral decisions in such circumstances. With its strong emphasis on the processes through which we behave ethically within a professional role the ethic of care offers some potential for a path through these challenges. It also potentially provides us with an ethical system sensitive to the impacts of gender. In acknowledging and emphasising our interdependence, our place within a matrix of relationships it is able to address power within the social worker/service user dyad and also contextualise this, by beginning to address the link between the localised experience of an individual and the broader structural impacts of gendered social relations. So the approach has the potential to engage with issues of latent power.

However this brings us to what a number of commentators have identified as a key weakness of this approach. With its single focus on gender it simplifies the complexity of identity with one single essentialist category over determining other types of difference. 'Oppositional discourses often extend the very relationships of domination that they are resisting' (Fawcett, Featherstone and Fook, 2004: 13) and when we consider the parent's social role ethnicity, sexuality, culture and social class for example, are all crucially important in its construction. An approach to ethics based on a narrative account of identity might offer some scope for addressing this issue (Wilks, 2005) but might also be susceptible to the other key criticism of the ethic of care, that although practice focused it is concerned with the particular, leaving us craving a more 'solid' universal understanding of ethics. It may however be that in conditions of uncertainty what we need to sacrifice the certainties of principlism and generalisability for an ethics closer to our lived professional experience.

Despite these criticisms both discourse ethics and the ethics of care make valid claims on having an important role in our understanding of the ethics of power. The focus of both these approaches is on the process through which we behave ethically in professional contexts. Given power's complexity and its intrusion into the relationships between social workers and service users, to understand it we need an ethical approach with a relational and communicative heart.

Conclusion

A danger of a process focus when thinking about the ethics of power is that being ethical simply equates to doing good social work well. We can see to a large extent how this is true. The General Social Care Council (GSCC) codes of practice enjoin practitioners to 'be accountable for the quality of their work and take responsibility for maintaining and improving their knowledge and skills' (GSCC, 2002). However the experience of practitioners is that good practice is not always a straightforward aspiration. External constraints impact upon our capacity to be the best practitioners we can be. In respect of the organisational context of practice it is possible to see how a stronger process focus can help anchor our practice when we are working in conditions of uncertainty and contexts where we are not the autonomous decision makers of traditional ethics. However there might be circumstances where the organisational context of social work made the sort of practice envisaged by the feminist ethic of care for example impossible, where for example 'the prioritisation of government targets over social work practice compromises social workers ability to operate ethically' (Ayre and Preston-Shoot, 2010). It also often seems as though discourse ethics and the ethics of care are premised upon the idea of cooperative service users, wiling recipients of good practice, which may also be some distance from the realities of social work in many settings.

Perhaps what they do offer us however, is a way of thinking about ethics which is more consistent with the demands of a critical and reflective approach to practice which requires a 'complex understanding of power' and 'a more complex practice of empowerment' (Fook, 2002). As we have seen these ethical approaches focused on communication have the potential to meet the needs of social workers practicing in complex and bureaucratic environments where the sources of power are diffuse. When we think about power it is so often the oppositional relationship between the care and control of individuals which occupies our attention. However social work itself, when allied to its commitment to social justice has the potential to be a powerful force for change for individuals, communities and society as a whole. The adoption of an ethics based around relationships and dialogue, which addresses the social context of practice, may be one way of supporting this neglected and sometimes lost aspect of social work's professional project.

References

Adams, R. (2003) *Social Work and Empowerment.* Basingstoke, Palgrave MacMillan.

Ayre, P. and Preston-Shoot, M. (2010) *Children's Services at the Crossroads.* Lyme Regis, Russell House Publishing.

Banks, S. (2004) *Ethics Accountability and The Social Professions.* Basingstoke, Palgrave MacMillan.

Banks, S. (2006) *Ethics and Values in Social Work.* Basingstoke, Palgrave MacMillan.

Beauchamp, T. (1994) The 'Four Principles' Approach. In Gillon, R. *Principles of Health Care Ethics.* Chichester, John Wiley.

Beauchamp, T. and Childress, (1994) The 'Four Principles' Approach. In Gillon, R. *Principles of Health Care Ethics.* Chichester, John Wiley.

Bowden, P. (1997) *Caring Gender Sensitive Ethics.* London, Routledge.

Carson, D. and Bain, C. (2008) *Professional Risk and Working With People: Decision Making in Health Social Care and Criminal Justice.* London, Jessica Kingsley.

Clark, C. (2000) *Social Work Ethics Politics, Principles and Practice.* Basingstoke, Macmillan.

Dominelli, L. (2002a) *Anti-oppressive Social Work Theory and Practice.* Basingstoke, MacMillan.

Dominelli, L. (2002b) *Feminist Social Work Theory and Practice.* Basingstoke, Palgrave.

Fawcett, B. and Featherstone, B. (2004) An Appraisal of The Notions of Post Modernism, Post Modernity and Post-Modern Feminism. In Fawcett, B., Featherstone, B. and Fook, J. *Practice and Research in Social Work, Post Modern Feminist Approaches.* London, Routledge.

Fook, J. (2002) *Social Work: Critical Theory and Practice.* London, Sage.

Foucault, M. (1980) *Power/Knowledge: Selected Interviews and Other Writings 1972–77.* Gordon, C. (Ed.) Brighton, Harvester.

Fraser, N. (1989) *Unruly Practices: Power, Discourse and Gender in Contemporary Theory.* Cambridge, Polity.

Garrett, P. (2009) Questioning Habermasian Social Work: A Note on Some Alternative Theoretical Resources. *British Journal of Social Work*, 39: 5, 867–83.

Gilligan, C. (1982) *In a Different Voice: Psychological Theory and Women's Development.* Cambridge, MA, Harvard University Press.

GSCC (2002) *Codes of Practice for Social Work.* London, GSCC.

Habermas, J. (1984) *Moral Consciousness and Communicative Action.* Cambridge, Polity.

Habermas, J. (1984) *The Theory of Communicative Action, Vol. 1.* Cambridge, Polity.

Habermas, J. (1987) *The Theory of Communicative Action, Vol. 2.* Cambridge, Polity.

Hayes, D. and Houston, S. (2007) Lifeworld and System and Family Group Conferences: Habermas's Contribution to Discourse in Child Protection. *British Journal of Social Work*, 37, 987–1006.

Holland, S. (2009) Looked After Children and The Ethic Of Care. *British Journal of Social Work*, Advance Access.

Houston, S. (2003) Establishing Virtue in Social Work: A Response to McBeath and Webb. *British Journal of Social Work*, 33: 6, 819–24.

Howe, D. (1994) Modernity Post-Modernity and Social Work. *British Journal of Social Work*, 24, 513–32.

Hugman, R. (2005) *New Approaches in Ethics for Caring Professions.* Basingstoke, Palgrave MacMillan.

Jones, C. (1983) *State Social Work and the Working Class.* Basingstoke, MacMillan.

Jones, C. (2001) Voices from the Front Line; State Social Work and New Labour. *British Journal of Social Work*, 31: 4, 547–62.

Juniper, J. (2008) Foucault and Spinoza: Philosophies of Immanence and The De-Centred Political Subject. *History of the Human Sciences*, 21: 2, 1–20.

Kohlberg, L. (1981) *Essays on Moral Development Vol.1.* San Francisco, Harper and Row.

Larrabee, M.J. (Ed.) (1993) *An Ethic of Care.* London, Routledge.

Lloyd, L. (2006) A Caring Profession? The Ethics of Care and Social Work with Older People. *British Journal of Social Work*, 36, 1171–85.

Lovat, T. and Gray, M. (2008) Towards a Proportionist Social Work Ethics: A Habermasian Perspective. *British Journal of Social Work*, 38, 1100–14.

McBeath, G. and Webb, S.A. (2002) Virtue Ethics and Social Work: Being Lucky, Realistic, and not Doing ones Duty. *British Journal of Social Work*, 32: 8, 1015–36.

Mills, S. (2003) *Michel Foucault.* Abingdon, Routledge.

Mullender, A. (2002) Persistent Oppressions. The Example of Domestic Violence. In Adams, R., Dominelli, L. and R. and Payne, M. (Eds.) *Critical Practice in Social Work*. Basingstoke, Palgrave MacMillan.

Orme, J. (2002) Social Work, Gender, Care and Justice. *British Journal of Social Work*, 32, 799–815.

Parsons, T. (1969) On the Concept of Political Power. In Bell, R., Edwards, D. and Wagner, R. (Eds.) *Political Power: A reader in Theory and Research*. New York, Free Press.

Parton, N. (1998) Risk, Advanced Liberalism and Child Welfare: The need to Rediscover Uncertainty and Ambiguity. *British Journal of Social Work*, 28, 5–27.

Parton, N. and Small, N. (1989) Violence, Social Work and the Emergence of Dangerousness. In Langan, M. and Lee, P. (Eds.) *Radical Social Work Today*. London, Unwin.

Rawls (1973) *A Theory of Justice*. Oxford, Oxford University Press.

Russel Day, P. (1981) *Social Work and Social Control*. London, Tavistock.

Sheppard, M. (2006) *Social Work and Social Exclusion*. Aldershot, Ashgate.

Smith Squire (2010) Social Workers Snatch Baby From Mother 'Not Clever Enough to Raise a Child' After She Flees to Ireland to Give Birth. *Daily Mail*, 22.1.10.

Smith, R. (2008) *Social Work and Power*. Basingstoke, MacMillan.

Thompson, N. (1993) *Anti-discriminatory Practice*. Basingstoke, MacMillan.

Tittle, P. (2005) *What if? . . . Collected Thought Experiments in Philosophy*. London, Pearson.

Tronto, J.C. (1993) *Moral Boundaries: A Political Argument for an Ethic of Care*. New York, Routledge.

Wilks, T. (2005) Social Work and Narrative Ethics. *British Journal of Social Work*, 35,1249–64.

CHAPTER 4

The Death of a Child: The Unavoidable Truth

Julia Stroud

Introduction

The publication of the details of the injuries and death of Baby P (Peter Connolly) in autumn 2008 led yet again to a public and political outpouring of horror and disgust over the violent deaths of children. A main theme in the extensive media reporting and public anger and was once more the perceived failings of professionals charged with safeguarding and preventing child deaths, particularly social workers and, to a lesser extent, medical practitioners. The public mood was summed by Rt. Hon. Ed Balls, then Secretary of State for Children, Schools and Families: 'The whole nation has been shocked and moved by the tragic and horrific death of Baby P. All of us find it impossible to comprehend how adults could commit such terrible acts of evil against this little boy. And the public is angry that nobody stepped in to prevent this tragedy from happening' (*The Guardian*, 1 December 2008). In March 2010, in his first annual report to Parliament and after details emerged of the circumstances of the death of Khyra Ishaq, the seven year old girl who was starved to death, the Chief Adviser on the Safety of Children stated: 'public interest and concern has not abated over the last twelve months; if anything both have increased especially in the wake of disturbing cases involving children' (Singleton, 2010: 6).

There is nothing new in the public's horror and anger. Writing in 1767, Erasmus Darwin identified, too, the extreme difficulty of comprehending how anyone, especially a parent, could inflict fatal harm on an child when he referred to the killing of an infant by its mother as 'this most unnatural crime' (King-Hele, 1981). The details of Peter Connolly's and Khyra Ishaq's sad and tragic deaths, like those of Victoria Climbié, Jasmine Beckford, Kimberley Carlisle, Maria Colwell and too many others, evidence parental/ carer violence and harm, completely at odds with the nurturing and caring responses which young, vulnerable children require. In the last two decades it has not been only the deaths of children within families (intra-familial child homicide) that provoke public horror. The murders of Jessica Chapman, Holly Wells and Sarah Payne by strangers and non-family members (extra-familial child homicide) have also led to public outcry. As Danson and Soothill (1996) have observed, the media coverage of stranger child homicides is more widespread than any other type of crime.

In our current, risk-averse society, there is a tendency to believe that all risk, including risk of child deaths, can be managed – if only social workers properly used their professional skills, followed procedures and exercised legal powers. The cries that, 'lessons must be learnt' and that 'something must be done' have become depressingly familiar refrains to social work practitioners charged with making difficult and challenging assessments and decisions in order to safeguard children. Political responses can reinforce erroneous public perceptions that zero risk childhoods are possible and that we can achieve certainty in an uncertain and complex world, where parents 'may be superficially compliant, evasive, deceitful, manipulative and untruthful' (LSCB Haringey, 2009: 24). In the wake of the death of Baby P, the Rt. Hon. Ed Balls' assertion: 'it is our duty to take whatever action is needed *to ensure that such a tragedy doesn't happen again*, that lessons are learned' (*The Guardian*, 12 November 2008 (emphasis added) evidences this. As Garrett (2009) has identified, a more balanced debate over the complexities of social work, safeguarding and child death began to emerge after the storm that followed publication of the details of Baby P's death. Further, the approach of the Social Work Task Force was measured, identifying the complexities, strengths and challenges of social work practice (Social Work Task Force, 2010). However, when details of Khyra Ishaq's death emerged during the trial of her mother and stepfather in February 2010, social workers were once again the focus of public anger, suggesting that the public desire to blame is deeply seated. Mrs. Justice King's statements from care proceedings, were widely reported: 'It is beyond belief that, in 2008 . . . a child of seven was withdrawn from school and thereafter kept in squalid conditions for a period of five months before finally dying of starvation' (*The Guardian*, 25 February 2010). It is within this environment of recrimination, anxiety and blame that social workers must assess and intervene where children are at risk of significant harm, the extreme consequence of which is child death.

Child death, policy and practice guidance

Over the last 35 years, child death has been a significant 'driver' of child care social work policy and practice in the United Kingdom. At the time of Maria Colwell's death practice was framed in the socio-medical discourse of the battered baby and non-accidental injury and then, in the era of the child abuse inquiries of the 1980s, as fatal child abuse. Since then, a socio-legal discourse of child protection and now safeguarding has been dominant in relation to child death (Parton, 2006). Ever more detailed practice guidance concerned with the assessment and monitoring of children suffering, or at risk of suffering significant harm, has been developed. This discourse with its procedural focus has assumed that assessments of such complex situations are a linear process. The predominance of the discourse can be seen post Baby P and Lord Laming's (2009) report, with the publication of a new version of *Working Together to Safeguard Children* (DCSF, 2010) which is 391 pages long, whereas the 1991 version comprised 126 pages (DoH, 1991). Procedural prescription has extended to time frames. For example, a core group meeting must take place within 10 working days of an initial child protection case conference and completion of the Core Assessment within 35 working days. The latter requirement has been a national indicator target. However, targets are not necessarily compatible with assessing complex family situations and can lead to 'inadequate' assessments (Singleton, 2010: 15). White et al. (2010) suggest that the focussing upon procedures, standards and timescales create conditions for error in practice and encourages social workers to try to limit the chances of being blamed if things go wrong. Independent review of the child protection system and, it appears of this approach, has been instigated by the Government based on three principles: early intervention; trusting professionals and removing bureaucracy so they can spend more of their time on the frontline; greater transparency and accountability. One question posed to the review is 'Have targets got in the way of good practice?' (Gove, 2010). It should be noted also that legalism has been dominant in relation to child murders committed by strangers. Stringent requirements for the registration and monitoring of sex offenders have been implemented through legislation (for example, *Sexual Offences Act 2003*) and via Multi-Agency Public Protection Arrangements (MAPPA) concerned with assessing and managing sexual and violent offenders, considered to pose a risk, or potential risk to children .

Within recent policy and practice guidance there has been an increased focus on child deaths, developed from 'Part Eight Reviews' (DoH, 1991) to Serious Case Reviews (SCR). *Working Together* (DCSF, 2006) introduced the requirement that Local Children Safeguarding Boards establish child death overview panels (CDOP) to review each child death with the aim of identifying whether a death should be classified as *preventable or potentially preventable* (emphasis added). Preventable child deaths are identified as 'those in which modifiable factors may have contributed to the death' (DCSF, 2010: 213) with a view to identifying 'any lessons to be learnt about how to safeguard and promote children's welfare in the future' (DCSF, 2010: 209). First data from these panels identifies that 2,000 deaths were reviewed 1 April 2008–31 March 2009 and that 110 were considered preventable (DCSF, 2009). However, the DCSF is rightly cautious about this data since LSCBs have found it difficult to interpret the definition of preventable child deaths and some panels have failed to reach a decision on the issue of whether complex child deaths were preventable (DCSF, 2009). Continuing this significant policy focus on child deaths, in June 2010 the Government issued guidance to Local Safeguarding Children Boards advising that Serious Case Review Reports, appropriately redacted and anonymised should be published 'to enable lessons to be learned from cases where a child dies or is seriously harmed or abuse or neglect is known' (Loughton, 2010).

Cooper (2005: 2) describes this dominant socio-legal discourse accurately as one of 'performance, behaviour and professional competence'. In relation to child death, the discourse ignores the fact that child death is an extremely interactive, complex and multi-faceted phenomenon (Bourget and Bradford, 1990; Stroud, 2008; Brandon et al., 2009). Further, a major effect is to move the focus away from the perpetrator who kills the child and their situation, characteristics and experiences (which information might inform future assessments) to the failures of systems and professionals, especially social workers. The discourse reinforces the popular and political belief that if only social workers 'policed' situations where children are at risk in accordance with established procedures, the tragic deaths of children would not happen again. This is a position which, of course, operates with the benefit of hindsight. It is suggested that the discourse with its associated procedural and performance management focus masks the complexities, challenges and difficulties facing social workers. In this contested environment it is important that evidence informs professional practice.

What do we know about child death?

The numerous public inquiries and serious case reviews of child deaths within families can give an impression that we have a detailed understanding of child death. This is misleading: individual serious case reviews and other inquiry reports can give in-depth information on the specific circumstances of specific, unique cases. Meta analyses of serious case reviews (e.g. Brandon et al., 2008; 2009) are developing some knowledge, although caution is needed as some serious case reviews fail to provide sufficient information to gain a 'clear understanding' of the circumstances surrounding the child's death (Brandon et al., 2009: 4). In particular, documents used in serious case reviews, which focus upon inter-agency working, may not provide in depth information on parents' or carers' histories, environment, psychological characteristics and relationship or attitude to the child (Stroud, 2008; Brandon et al., 2009).

The interrogation of child death might be said to have been subsumed under the concept of fatal child abuse and the socio-legal discourse of safeguarding. In fact, child death is rarely examined or reviewed in its entirety (Stanton et al., 2000; Brookman and Macguire, 2003; Dolan et al., 2003; Stroud, 2008). In part this relates to the range of sub-groups and different terms that are used (Stroud, 2008). Fatal child abuse is the term often applied to *all* child deaths but should be used only in relation to the specific pattern of assaults associated with child abuse (punching, shaking, hitting, striking occurring over time), which pattern has been evidenced so tragically in the deaths of Baby P and Victoria Climbié. This pattern of assault is not relevant generally to the killing of a child by strangers or to children killed by a parent or carer experiencing acute mental illness, where the assault is of a different nature and may relate to stabbing, strangulation, smothering (Reder and Duncan, 1999; Stroud, 2008). The widely reported cases of John Hogan, who killed his six year old son in Crete by jumping off a balcony and of Alberto Izago who killed his two year old daughter while acutely psychotic are examples. Yet Brandon et al. (2009: 9) in discussing child death, continue to refer to 'deaths from *child abuse* worldwide'.

Filicide is a term which refers to the killing of a child by a parent. In England and Wales infanticide has a specific legal definition, referring to the killing of a child under one year by its mother, whose mind was 'disturbed' at the time of the offence by reason of not having fully recovered from the effect of giving birth (*Infanticide Act 1938*). Neonaticide was a term first used by Resnick (1970) and refers to the killing of a child on the day of its birth. Child homicide covers all the preceding terms and embraces all types of assaults: it includes the killing of a child by its parents or carers (intra familial child homicide) or by strangers (extra familial child homicide). Child homicide includes the common law offences of murder, manslaughter and 's2 manslaughter', i.e. where the defendant suffered from 'abnormality of mind' at the time of the killing (s2 *Homicide Act 1957*).

Development of classification of child death by motives has been a focus in the psychiatric and criminological literatures (for example, Bourget and Bradford, 1990; Wilczynski, 1997; Dolan et al., 2003). However, confusions can arise from these systems. For example, the classification 'altruistic' includes the mercy killing of a severely ill or dying child by its parent and the killing of a child by a depressed or suicidal parent. Most recently, Brandon et al., (2009: 132) have proposed a framework for categorising different types of fatal child maltreatment, recognising child deaths 'do not form one homogenous group' and propose six categories, including infanticide or covert homicide; severe physical assaults; extreme neglect or deprivational abuse; deliberate or overt homicide. Such frameworks and systems rely on retrospective analysis of motive and the projection of the researcher into the situation and for these reasons they may be unreliable. Further, analysis of motive does not have a focus on the broad spectrum of the child, parent's and family's situation, history, environment and the quality of relationships. Such classification, therefore, may not necessarily assist or inform assessments. However, our underdeveloped knowledge about child death and of those who kill children may reflect also the challenging and the very difficult nature of the phenomenon. Wilczynski (1997: 11) uses the word 'taboo' in relation to child death.

Incidence

The nature and extent of the media coverage of all types of child homicides, together with the growing policy and practice guidance on child death and safeguarding, gives the impression that the number of children being killed each year is increasing. Such impressions are reinforced politically when ministers erroneously refer to 'thousands of children dying each year' (Ed Balls, *House of Commons Hansard Debates*, 20 November 2008). In reality, child homicide is still a rare phenomenon (Stanton et al., 2000; Pritchard, 2002) although we do not know precisely how many children are killed each year. To an extent this is because child death statistics, with different reporting and recording criteria, are found in a range of data sets (WHO Standardised Mortality Statistics; Home Office Statistical Bulletins, Homicides, Firearm Offences and Intimate Violence; ONS Mortality Statistics).

Home Office statistics, based on cases recorded by the police, are preferred to assess the incidence of child death because there is clear evidence that homicide has taken place, also comparisons against same criteria are possible over 30 years. Home Office homicide statistics (Smith et al., 2010) covering the offences of murder, manslaughter, infanticide, identify that in 2008/9, 50 children are currently recorded as having been victims of homicide (7.7 per cent of all 651 homicides). 70 per cent of children and young people under 16 knew their killer, with 56 per cent being killed by a parent. In only two cases were children known to have been killed by a stranger. For other child deaths there are currently no suspects, though this is likely to fall as investigations continue. Using Home Office data the average number of child homicides annually between 1998/9 and 2004/5 is 74. These years have been chosen because of the possibility that in later years there may still be cases which are unresolved. While each child death represents a child who has suffered trauma and the tragic loss of a young life, it is clear that child deaths are not increasing or out of control.

Pritchard and Williams (2010) using WHO mortality statistics, have asserted that violent child abuse deaths (children 0–14 years) reduced by 60 per cent between 1974 and 2006. Conversely, Creighton and Tissier (2003) consider that while child homicide statistics fluctuate each year, the overall rate for England and Wales has remained broadly similar since the 1970s. Of course caution is needed because it is likely that that there are a number of unrecorded child homicides each year (i.e. deaths where the cause of death was uncertain but may relate to abuse, neglect or other assault). Wilczynski (1997) has proposed this could increase the number of child deaths to over 300 per year. Home Office statistics again demonstrate that child homicide is mainly an intra-familial phenomenon with killings by parents committed in roughly equal proportions by mothers and fathers (Brookman and Maguire, 2003). When strangers or acquaintances (extra-familial child homicide) are perpetrators a sexual assault often precedes the homicide (Somander and Rammer, 1991;

Stroud and Pritchard, 2001). While children as a whole have a low risk of being killed compared to adults, infants aged one year and under have been identified consistently as being most at risk of being killed (Smith et al., 2010; Brookman and Maguire, 2003). This risk to young infants has been found across all studies (for example, d'Orban, 1979; Falkov, 1996). Brandon et al. (2009) studying serious case reviews for 189 children (two thirds of whom died) found half were less than a year old and over two thirds of the children were under five years . Older children and young people who died were 'hard to help' and suicide was a significant factor.

It is important to put the average incidence of 74 child homicides per year into context. In 2008 in England and Wales a total of 6,214 children aged 0–15 years died (ONS, 2010). Many deaths in childhood are the expected consequence of congenital health problems and disease. For example, cancer accounted for 20 per cent of the deaths of children aged 1–15 years (ONS, 2010). The mortality rate for children has consistently declined with ONS identifying a 6 per cent reduction for children aged 1–14 years between 1980 and 2008. Further, in comparison to child homicide statistics, in 2008 a total of 2,807 children died or were seriously injured on the roads, with 124 children dying (Department of Transport, 2009).

Society, then, tolerates a range of risks to children that are higher than that of child homicide; in the case of child road deaths and injuries perhaps this is because using a car suits our collective convenience. Yet the strong emotions surrounding child death and the public and political expectation that social workers will manage and control child killings have continued unabated now for several decades. It is suggested that this could be because the type of violence reported in the media (especially of stranger child murders) undermines confidence in usual precautions against harm and inspires fear, emphasising the vulnerability and helplessness of victims and the ruthlessness or recklessness of perpetrators (Floud and Young, 1981). It is easier to identify with the child victims than ever consider ourselves as potential aggressors – as the person who loses control with a child. Human beings like to feel in control and like predictability it may be easier to project collective fears of being out of control, for whatever reason, on to the perpetrator and to deal with our emotions also by blaming social workers.

Research evidence

Practitioners looking for research evidence on child death to inform their practice will find that studies are published intermittently in the psychiatric, criminology and, of course, child abuse literature. In part, the intermittent nature of research publications reflects the fact that child homicide is statistically rare, is considered in terms of sub groups rather than as an entity and also reflects the fact that it is difficult to find unselected case samples (Stroud, 2008).

Further, there are challenges in accessing data, because of confidentiality, ethical and legal processes (Wlczynski, 1997; Stroud, 2008). Thus, many studies use small case samples or relate to particular sub groups. For example, Bourget and Bradford (1990) studied 13 filicides referred to a Canadian forensic psychiatric service over eight years; Simpson and Stanton (2000) five maternal filicides similarly referred in New Zealand and Stroud and Pritchard (2001) 27 child homicides committed in two English counties over ten years. In terms of larger samples, Dolan et al. (2003) studied 64 male suspects charged with child homicide and remanded in HMP Leeds, whereas d'Orban (1979) studied 89 female suspects so charged and remanded in HMP Holloway. Statistical research has been dominant with a concern for classifications and the incidence of psychiatric disorders. There has been little qualitative research (Stanton et al., 2000; Stroud, 2008) which may afford greater understanding of the precursors of child homicide, in terms of the experiences of perpetrators, their circumstances, psychological state and relationship to the child.

Studies have repeatedly found that a significant proportion of those who kill a child experience mental health problems, with the following identified: puerperal mental illness; depression; schizophrenia and psychotic states and personality disorders, including dissocial personality disorder/ psychopathy (Bourget and Bradford, 1990; Falkov, 1996; Resnick, 1969; Stroud, 2008). As an example, Kyra Ishaq's mother was found to be suffering depression at the time of her child's death and the court accepted her plea of manslaughter on grounds of diminished responsibility. The violent assaults committed by those who killed Baby P and Victoria Climbié reflect psychological difficulties in relation to impulse control, low threshold for discharge of violence and the 'callous unconcern' for others which are the hallmark of dissocial or psychopathic disorder (*ICD 10*. WHO, 1992: 204) although serious case reviews rarely identify the perpetrator's psychological functioning in this way. Falkov (1996: 8) reviewed 100 'Part Eight reviews' concerned with parental filicide and found clear evidence of 'psychiatric morbidity' in 32 cases. As he was using childcare documents, 23 reviews had 'insufficient documentation' for inclusion and 45 had no psychiatric details recorded, so the 32 cases may be an underestimation. d'Orban (1979) found that only 18 of the 89 women remanded in Holloway (20 per cent) had no mental disorder when they killed. Somander and Rammer (1991) in their study of all 79 child homicides in Sweden 1971–1980 reported that only 10 out of 77 perpetrators identified were not found to have a mental disorder when examined by a psychiatrist after the offence. Stroud and Pritchard (2001) found 12 of 27 perpetrators were mentally ill at the time of the offence and Dolan et al. (2003) in their study of men remanded in HMP Leeds, found 30 of 63 had a mental disorder, still significant though lower proportions than in d'Orban's all female sample.

Research evidences the assertion that child homicide is a complex, intricate and heterogeneous phenomenon (Bourget and Bradford, 1990). As well as identifying the importance of mental health factors, research identifies that perpetrators experience a range of psychosocial difficulties described variously as 'stress' (d'Orban, 1979: 563) 'socio-economic adversity' (Falkov, 1996: 18) and 'multiple problems of various kinds' (Wilczynski, 1997: 101). In their biennial analyses of Serious Case Reviews, Brandon et al. (2008; 2009) have found that nearly three quarters of children lived with past or present parental domestic violence, mental health or substance misuse, with these characteristics often co-existing. Further, nearly half the families lived in poor conditions, moved frequently and had poor or negative family support.

A study of 68 child deaths inquired into these factors in an attempt to understand the interplay between the perpetrators' psychological condition and their psychosocial environment (Stroud, 2008). Sixty eight individuals who had been charged with a child homicide or attempt were studied; there were 70 offences since two individuals were convicted of both a homicide and an attempt during the period of the study. 69 children died and 19 survived attempts. Data from forensic pre-trial assessments for court were accessed via medium and high forensic mental health settings. The majority of perpetrators (84 per cent) experienced multiple and severe ongoing adversities in childhood. Such experiences are known to predispose to later psychological problems and difficulties in functioning with a reduced ability to understand and respond appropriately and sensitively to their own children's needs (Rutter, 1999; Sadowski, 1999; Howe, 2005). Individuals' experiences of childhood adversity included all forms of abuse and neglect, separation from parents and witnessing parental discord and violence. Further, individuals experienced frequent changes of environment. In adulthood, high levels of psychological and mental health difficulties were found with delusional beliefs being the most common (44 per cent). Twelve per cent of cases reflected the pattern of assaults found in child abuse. The perpetrators' adult lives were found to mirror their disturbed and unsettled childhoods. Adults experienced difficult, violent, broken and conflictual relationships (60 per cent) or lived in isolation (32 per cent), with poor levels of contact and support. Data sheds light on areas for social workers to consider in assessments. For example, difficulties in relationships could be subtle, in 38 per cent of cases family and partners did not understand mental ill health and did not pick up on, or respond to, perpetrators' increasing mental distress. In 51 per cent of cases perpetrators repeatedly sought help for their difficulties but were unsuccessful, because, for example, they sought help from the wrong sources (e.g. from housing departments, the police, churches). In 51 per cent of cases the perpetrator had a difficult relationship with the child (e.g. because of over identification of the child; the child being born as a result of sexual assault) and 37 per cent of victims were born as the result of unplanned pregnancies (Stroud, 2008).

Social workers need to be alert to issues of parental/carer stress in relation to risk of child death. Individuals' difficulties and stress interacted with the onset and relapse of different forms of mental disorder and/ or worsened psychological functioning. Nearly all individuals studied had stressful lives. Providing an account of the stress is challenging because of the heterogeneity of different experiences and because of the interactive nature of the processes. However, the following suggests a framework for understanding how stress may be understood in relation to child death. Ninety per cent of individuals had *'stressful life contexts'* – a summative category which included all ongoing, long term stress; e.g. psychological problems, relationship problems, isolation, long term effects of migration. Seventy eight per cent experienced *'meaningful experiences'* – stressful experiences to which perpetrators ascribed a particular meaning (e.g. birth of a child, unemployment; bereavement) and which individuals identified as acting as 'change points', worsening functioning and psychological well-being. An increase in stress close to the offence in time (from a month to hours) was found in 45 per cent of cases. The category *'and then something happened'*, reflects the sense that individuals were *just* managing to care for the child until some extra stress occurred. Even in the 10 per cent of cases where there was no long term stress, there was some unexpected stress shortly before the offence. Examples included being the victim of a partner's violence or hostility; being left alone and the anniversaries of deaths, marriages (Stroud, 2008). Greenland (1987) proposed that there could be a 'trigger' for an assault on a child, but this is too linear a notion, for it does not take account of the interaction with the individual's psychological state nor the importance of relationships, isolation and role of support. It is suggested that exploring the psychological state, mental health, functioning and psychosocial experiences of those who kill a child, sets out the complex experiences of parents and carers who kill a child. By exploring these different aspects the challenges in terms of prevention becomes clearer.

Summary and conclusion

Child death is a complex phenomenon in which multiple factors in relation to the perpetrator's situation interact with each other prior to the offence. The individual's 'internal world', their psychological state, cognitive processes, histories, current and past relationships and stressful experiences appear to be key (Stroud, 2008). Those charged with preventing significant harm and child death work in what has become a politicised arena and under intense and hostile public and media scrutiny. Further, practice has been guided by increasingly demanding procedures where requirements as to timescales, targets and performance management may militate against the complex analyses required in assessments. Within practice guidance there has been an increased focus child death and upon 'learning lessons' from Serious Case Reviews (DCSF, 2010; Loughton, 2010). However, the extent to which this can be achieved and child deaths prevented is very unclear (Falkov,

1996). For example, in a substantial number of cases children and their families are not known to statutory services. In Stroud's (2008) study focusing on perpetrators' psychological state and psychosocial experiences, 53 per cent of individuals had prior contact with mental health services, but 47 per cent had not. In Brandon et al.'s (2009) biennial review of Serious Case Reviews, only 17 per cent of the children were currently subject to a child protection plan with a further 11 per cent having been the subject of a plan in the past. As Brandon et al. (2009: 10) put it, child death may well not be typical of safeguarding practice and 'the recurring nature of child death calls into question the extent to which lessons can be learnt and child death prevented'.

Within the increased policy and practice focus on child death there has been particular attention paid to problems in safeguarding systems, interagency working and practice failings (see, for example, Rose and Barnes, 2008). While there has been increased attention paid to professional practice and judgment, there remains concern with interagency practice (Gove, 2010). This focus does not engage with the details and interactive complexities of individual perpetrators' lives and the circumstances and events leading up to a child's death. However, there have been recent attempts to engage with this interplay of factors. Fish et al. (2008) proposed the use of systems theory in relation to Serious Case Review processes and, building on this, Brandon et al. (2009) have used an ecological model in their most recent biennial analyses. Gilbert at al. (2009: 11) identify that an ecological model 'conceptualises maltreatment as multiply determined by forces at work in the individual, in the family, and in the community'. These are positive developments for they offer the crucial perspective of engaging dynamically with individuals' emotional histories, own experiences of parenting, relationships, cognitive models and current stressors, all of which may affect their current psychological state and functioning and safe care of children.

Further, there has been increased recognition of the importance of relationships in social work practice and how a relationship between a client and a professional may be influential in assessment of, and engagement with, long-standing social, emotional and interpersonal problems. Equally, there has been recognition of how histories are important in understanding individuals' situations (Cooper, 2005; Howe, 2005). This is important: relationships, histories, causation and understanding of uncertainty and complexity may be said to have been at odds with the recent procedurally driven focus of much child care social work practice guidance. The childhood and life experiences of those who kill a child indicate that an increased focus on these areas is important in practice.

The decisions which social workers are required to make in child protection are rarely 'clear cut or risk free' and social workers are not 'infallible' (Singleton, 2010: 7). It has to be acknowledged that there have been a small number of child deaths where social workers have failed to assess properly and intervene and, as a result, children have died. This has led to review of social work practice, which has, to an extent, highlighted the competing discourses within social work practice itself. This was brought to the fore in the second Serious Case Review on Baby P (LSCB Haringey, 2009). Social work has embraced rightly a discourse of empowerment, equality, partnership and joint working with parents and families. LCSB Haringey point out, however, the potential limits of this discourse in safeguarding practice; for example, in terms of a focus upon parental strengths (use of Solution Focussed Brief Therapy) and upon partnership working (placement of children with family and friends). The challenge for social work now is to retain both its commitment to equality and empowerment and maintain high level of knowledge of relevant theory and research evidence. I would suggest that the maintenance of social work skills and knowledge together with well-developed practice skills is what is needed to inform and support assessment of, and engagement with, those who pose a serious risk to children.

Child death is a phenomenon which has existed across time. Over the last 30 years the incidence of child death has been stable and, given the unique circumstances of each case, it is questionable to what extent child death can be prevented or predicted further (Falkov, 1996; Brandon et al., 2009). The Chief Adviser on the Safety of Children sums up the current position: 'Agencies involved in safeguarding believe that government activity now needs to change focus from guidelines and prescription to supporting professional practice' (Singleton, 2010: 4). In my view such a focus will have the greatest benefit to all children who may be at risk.

References

Balls, E. (2008) Ed Balls' statement in full. *The Guardian*, 1 December. Basingstoke: Palgrave.

Bourget, D. and Bradford, J. (1990) Homicidal Parents. *Canadian Journal of Psychiatry*. 35: 233–8.

Brandon, M. et al (2009) *Understanding Serious Case Reviews and their Impact. A Biennial Analysis of serous Case Reviews 2005–7*. London: DCSF.

Brandon, M. et al. (2008) *Analysing Child Deaths and Serious Injury through Abuse and Neglect: What Can we Learn? A Biennial Analysis of Serious Case Reviews 2003–2005*. London: DCSF.

Brookman, F. and Macguire, M. (2003) *Reducing Homicide: A Review of the Possibilities*. London: HMSO.

Carter, H. (2010) Failures That Led to Mother Starving Khyra Ishaq to Death 'Beyond Belief'. *The Guardian*, 25 February.

Cooper, A. (2005) Surface and Depth in the Victoria Climbié Report. *Child and Family Social Work*, 10: 1–9.

Creighton, S.J. and Tissier, G. (2003) *Child Killings in England and Wales.* London: NSPCC.

d'Orban, P. (1979) Women Who Kill Their Children. *British Journal of Psychiatry*, 134: 560–71.

Danson, L. and Soothill, K. (1996) Child Murder and The Media: A Study of The Reporting of Child Murder. in The Times 1887–1990. *Journal of Forensic Psychiatry*, 7: 3, 495–503.

DCSF (2006) *Working Together to Safeguard Children. A Guide to Inter-Agency Working to Safeguard and Promote The Welfare of Children.* London: DCSF.

DCSF (2009) *Statistical Release. Preventable Child Deaths in England: Year Ending 31 March 2009.* London: DCSF.

DCSF (2010) *Working Together to Safeguard Children. A Guide to Inter-Agency Working to Safeguard and Promote the Welfare of Children.* London: DCSF.

Dept of Transport (2009) *Road Casualties in Britain: Main Results 2008.* accessed 31 March 2010 [http://www.dft.gov.uk/pgr/statistics/datatablespublications/accidents/casualtiesmr/rcgbmainresults2008].

DoH (1991) *Working Together Under the Children Act 1989.* London, DoH.

Dolan, M. et al. (2003) Child Homicide. *Medicine, Science and the Law*, 43: 2 153–69.

Falkov, A. (1996) *Study of Working Together 'Part 8' Reports. Fatal Child Abuse and Psychiatric Disorder: An Analysis of 100 Area Child Protection Committee Case Reviews.* London: DoH.

Fish, S. et al. (2008) Learning Together to Safeguard Children: Developing a Multi-Agency Systems Approach For Case Reviews. (SCIE Guide 24). [http://www.scie.org.uk/publications/guides/guide24/index.asp], accessed 31 March 2010.

Floud, J. and Young, W. (1981) *Dangerousness and Criminal Justice.* London: Heinemann.

Garrett, P.M. (2009) The case of 'Baby P': Opening up Spaces For Debate on The 'Transformation' of Children's Services? *Critical Social Policy*, 29; 533–47.

Gilbert, R. et al. (2009) Burden and Consequences of Child Maltreatment in High Income Countries. *The Lancet*, 373: 68–81.

Glendenning, L. and Tran, M. (2008) Balls Orders Urgent Enquiry Into Baby P Case. *The Guardian*, 12 November.

Gove, M. (2010) Munro Review of Child Protection Better Frontline Services to Protect Children. Letter from Rt Hon Michael Gove to Professor Eileen Munro 10 June 2010. www.education.gov.uk/news/news.munroreview

Greenland, C. (1987) *Preventing C.A.N. Deaths.* London: Tavistock.

House of Commons (2008) *Hansard Debates*, 29 November 2008. London: The Stationery Office

Howe, D. (2005) *Child Abuse and Neglect: Attachment, Development and Intervention.* London: Palgrave.

King-Hele, D. (Ed.) (1981) *The Letters of Erasmus Darwin.* Cambridge: Cambridge University Press.

Lord Laming (2009) *The Protection of Children in England: A Progress Report.* London: HMSO.

Loughton, T. (2010) Publication of Serious Case Review Overview Reports and Munro Review of Child Protection. Letter from Tim Loughton MP, Parliamentary Under Secretary of State for Children and Families to LSCb Chairs; Directors of Children's Services. www.eduction.gov.uk/news/news/munroreview

LSCB Haringey (2009) *Serious Case Review: Baby Peter. Executive Summary.* London: LCSB Haringey.

Office of National Statistics (2010) *Childhood, Infant and Perinatal Mortality in England and Wales, 2008.* Newport: ONS.

Ofsted (2008) *The Annual Report of her Majesty's Chief Inspector of Education, Children's Services and Skills.* London: DCSF.

Parton, N. (2006) *Safeguarding Children; Early Intervention and Surveillance in Late Modern Society.*

Pritchard, C. (2002) Children's Homicide and Road Deaths in England and Wales and the USA: An International Comparison 1974–1997. *British Journal of Social Work.* 32: 495–502.

Pritchard, C. and Williams, R. (2010) Comparing Possible 'Child Abuse Related Deaths' in England and Wales With The Major Developed Countries 1974–2006. *British Journal of Social Work* (forthcoming).

Reder, P. and Duncan, S. (1999) *Lost Innocents. A Follow-Up Study of Fatal Child Abuse.* London:

Resnick, P. (1969) Child murder by parents: A psychiatric review of filicide. *American Journal of Psychiatry* 126: 325–334.

Resnick, P. (1970) Murder of the Newborn: A Psychiatric Review of Neonaticide. *American Journal of Psychiatry*, 126: 1414–20.

Rose, W. and Barnes, J. (2008) *Improving Safeguarding Practice: A Study of Serious Case Reviews 2001–2003.* London: DCSF/Open University.

Rutter, M. (1999) Psychosocial Adversity and Child Psychopathology. *British Journal of Psychiatry*, 174: 480–93.

Sadowski, H. et al. (1999) Early Life Family Disadvantages and Major Depression in Adulthood. *British Journal of Psychiatry*, 12: 233–60.

Simpson, A. and Stanton, J. (2000) Maternal Filicide: A Reformulation of Factors Relevant to Risk. *Criminal Behaviour and Mental Health.* 10: 136–47.

Singleton, P. (2010) *The Chief Adviser on the Safety of Children. First Annual Report to Parliament.* London: DCSF.

Smith, K. (Ed.) et al. (2010) *Home Office Statistical Bulletin. Homicide, Firearm Offences and Intimate Violence 2008/9.* London: Home Office.

Social Work Taskforce (2009) *Building a Safe Confident Future. The Final Report of the Social Work Taskforce.* London: DCSF.

Somander, L. and Rammer, L. (1991) Intra- and Extra-Familial Child Homicide in Sweden 1971–1980. *Child Abuse and Neglect,* 15: 44–55.

Stanton, J., Simpson, A. and Wouldes, T. (2000) A Qualitative Study of Filicide By Mentally Ill Mothers. *Child Abuse and Neglect,* 24: 11, 1451–60.

Stroud, J. (2008) A Psychosocial Analysis of Child Homicide. *Critical Social Policy,* 28: 4, 482–505.

Stroud, J. and Pritchard, C. (2001) Child Homicide, Psychiatric Disorder and Dangerousness: A Review and an Empirical Approach. *British Journal of Social Work,* 31: 249–69.

White S. et al. (2010) *Error, Blame and Responsibility in Child Welfare: Problematics of Governance in an Invisible Trade.* www.esrcsocietytoday.ac.uk/ESRCInfoCentre/Plain_English_summaries/envir...

WHO (1992) *The ICD 10. Classification of Mental and Behavioural Disorders.* Geneva: WHO.

Wilczynski, A. (1997) *Child Homicide.* London: Greenwich Medical Media.

CHAPTER 5

Reformulating the Rule of Optimism

Toyin Okitikpi

Throughout my investigations it has been clear that the vast majority of people working in this area aspire to improve the lives of the most vulnerable children and young people.

Lord Laming, 2009

Introduction

To some extent there has been a conspiracy of silence in two areas of social work, both of which have profound effect on the practice of social work. Firstly the rule of optimism (which is the focus of this chapter) continues to play a major role in the way practitioners approach children and families and individuals with whom they are involved. Secondly the social work profession is often reluctant to be explicit about the nature and extent of its powers. This chapter attempts to explore both of these areas, not in an attempt to merely highlight their shortcomings, but rather to discuss ways in which they could be reconsidered and reformulated in order to enhance practice.

Generally practitioners often make reference to conducting an assessment, intervening in the family, accommodating children, or going to court in order to obtain a particular order. None of these terms convey the underlying reality that the practitioner's actions are governed by quite strong legal powers. In fact there is very little explicit acknowledgement of how their power is exercised in such instances. In place of an open discussion with society and service users about the scope of social work powers there is a void filled by misinformation and half-truths. Such coyness fuels the perception that social work is a law onto itself, making decisions about people's lives without consulting with others and working in a cloak of secrecy. While practitioners do their very best to play down, or even ignore, the controlling (power) element of their role service users are much more acutely aware of it. Although services users may not have a clear understanding of the range of social work powers nevertheless they have a sense of its potential impact. This would go some way to explain

61

why, despite the difficulties or problems they may be experiencing, they would try to avoid, at all cost, contact with social services and social workers. Having a social worker involved in one's family life could of course be a positive experience but it could also be a negative one inducing a feeling of helplessness and powerlessness. It is accepted that power operates at different levels, both structural and individual, and while a practitioner may, through their role, possess certain legal powers, the (positional versus personal) power balance may be experienced differently when other factors are taken into consideration. Both Mandell (2008) and Smith (2008) in their different ways, acknowledged the complexities and dynamics involved in the use of self and power within the context of the professional relationship.

On the whole the social work profession has never really been comfortable with being associated with, and viewed as, just another arm of the state with the capacity to exercise power over others. Instead they have been at pains to emphasise their anti-oppressive approach and their enabling and 'empowering' role. A point reinforced by Horner (2003: 2) who suggests that: 'The social work profession promotes social change, problem solving in human relationships and the empowerment and liberation to enhance well-being'.

Power, as contained in the legal rules, is generally viewed with suspicion at best and as an unnecessary distraction from being able to develop the kind of relationship that would facilitate the desired change in the service user. Far from seeing the power contain within their role as benign, they generally view holding such powers as reinforcing the divide between themselves and service users and further contributing to people's sense of powerlessness.

Evidence suggests that there is a great deal of uncertainty and lack of knowledge by practitioners of the legal rules that govern their work (Sheppard, 1996; Ofsted, 2009). Moreover practitioners themselves have been honest in acknowledging that they lack confidence and competence to use their legal powers in practice (Braye and Preston-Shoot, 2009). While lack of competence and confidence may provide some explanation for social workers' lack of application of their legal powers, I would also suggest that the very nature of social work training and the ethos and ideals that are at the core of the profession encourages control-adverse mindset. It was Colby (2007) who proclaimed that social work is a remarkable profession and, for many in the profession, it is therefore not surprising that there should be a long queue of people wanting to join its ranks.

People decide to enter the social work profession for many different reasons. For some it is an opportunity to challenge and try to redress the iniquity that exists in society. It is also a way of helping those who are caught in the maelstrom of a brutish capitalist system. For others it is about 'doing some good' by working with people to help them find a better way of coping with the difficulties and problems that affect their lives. For many others there are combinations of reasons and different factors that make it difficult to characterise their motivation in such simplistic terms. Those who do enter social work are often confronted, at a fairly stage, with the duality (care and control) contained within the role. Unsurprisingly while most people are familiar with the caring aspects of being a social worker, less clearly understood is the controlling element of the role. As O'Brian (2003: 389) perceptively observed 'The social worker as facilitator of change or agent of social control epitomises this struggle for social work identity'.

People within the profession know that social workers do not make decisions that involve, for example, removing a child from their parents or carers in isolation. In reality the involvement of other professionals is generally viewed as an important element in the decision making process. In fact social workers do not have independent powers to remove a child without the sanction of the courts (see Chapter 2 and Chapter 9 of this volume) or in some cases, the support of the police. The overriding consideration of practitioners is to act in the best interest of those that they are most concerned about and this may in fact involve taking actions that may seem, on the face of it, contrary to the idea of helping, caring and supporting. The idea of exerting such power over service users is generally viewed as an anathema in social work circles. As Smith (2008: 17) rightly noted 'at one and the same time, acutely aware of their own relative powerlessness in an organisational and structural sense, and yet concerned as to how to manage their own authority over service users'.

Essentially the duality contained within the role is generally perceived as a binary, *care versus* control, rather than *care **and** control*. The difference between 'versus' and 'and' is more than mere semantics since the expectation is that to care, in some cases, may involve having to exert control. Taking such action will inevitably affect the professional relationship that may have been developed as well as any trust that has been carefully nurtured over time. Social workers are, in the main, schooled in seeing the positives in people and they are encouraged to work in a way that does not stigmatise, oppress, discriminate or reinforce the marginalisation that is the daily experiences of people involved with social welfare and social work. Also, I would argue that, the tendency to see the positives in others is not only borne out of the desire not to discriminate but also due to an uncomplicated interpretation of what it means, as social worker, to have power to intervene in other people's lives. While practitioners are comfortable with the caring aspects of their role they are uncomfortable at exercising their authority or exerting control (Beckett, 2009; Braye and Preston-Shoot, 2009).

Tew's (2006) analysis of power is helpful in this instance because, as he makes clear, power within the context of the professional relationship is far more complex and multi-dimensional in nature. According to Tew there are at least three different ways in which power is and could be exercised. For example there is ***power to*** (assess or investigate) ***power together*** (collaboration, working in partnership, re-establishment of safety or homeostasis) and ***power over*** (removing into a place of safety, accommodating). These points are discussed in some depth by Amanda Thorpe in this volume, Chapter 7.

What emerges from Tew's analysis is that rather than viewing power as a lineal notion that could only be interpreted as *power over* it should be seen that different kinds of power are being exercised throughout the intervention. In other words there are different types of power in operation during every contact and encounter between the practitioner and the service user. The important point is to recognise how power operates and to develop a deeper level of understanding of its application in practice. It is within this context that a reconsideration of the rules of optimism becomes important.

The rule of optimism

Social workers operate with greater accountability within a relatively tight structure encompassing frameworks, criteria, thresholds and clearly defined guidelines. However, what has been interesting to observe is that despite the plethora of reforms, and a practice ethos that has devalued relationship building, many practitioners still rely too readily or fall back too easily on the rule of the optimism. Many of the social inquiry reports into deaths of children have consistently highlighted practitioners' overreliance on the rule of optimism and their adult focused approach when working with vulnerable children that have been identified as cause for concern.

It is widely acknowledge that it was Dingwall, Eeklaar and Murray (1983) in their publication *The Protection of Children – State Intervention and Family Life*, who first coined the phrase **Rule of Optimism**. The term was coined because they found that social workers tend not to apportion any blame to parents. They found that workers hardly made any allegations of mistreatment of children by their parents, even in situations where there were problems and major concerns. They describe this attitude as the product of the 'rule of optimism' in that staffs are required, if possible, to think the best of parents. Blom-Cooper (1985) noted that Dingwall, Eeklaar and Murray, attributed social workers' positive perception of parents attitude and behaviour towards their children for two reasons. Firstly practitioners are influenced by (a) cultural relativism; and (b) the assumption that parents are imbued with instinctive and natural love for their children. According to Blom-Cooper (1985: 216):

> *The former is an intellectual position that all cultures are an equally valid way of formulating relationships between human beings and between human beings and the material world. Members of one culture 'have no right to criticise members of another by importing their own standards of judgement'. The latter is derived from the belief that parent/child life is 'an institutional phenomenon grounded in human nature.*

However in his view: 'If it is assumed that all parents love their children as a fact of nature, then it becomes very difficult to read evidence in a way which is inconsistent with this assumption' (ibid.).

To some extent it is understandable why social workers fall into the rule of optimism trap. As practitioners they have been schooled in seeing social work as a transformative, facilitative, supportive, educative and caring profession. Its main goals are to improve people's lives and help them to rediscover, adapt or develop new ways of coping with their difficulties and problems. The profession see itself as a change agent capable of enabling people to deal with whatever difficulty may have befallen them. While recipients of social work services may be viewed negatively by society at large practitioners see it as their duty not to label people negatively or input malicious intensions on their actions. Social workers pride themselves on not stigmatising nor perpetuating the negative stereotypical assumptions associated with being a service user. Rather they believe in seeing people as human beings first and foremost preferring to highlight positive attributes rather than dwell on the negative aspects of people's lives or behaviour. Although the rule of optimism is a value laden concept I would argue that it is borne out of the same humanitarian ideals that underlie the practice of social work. It is compatible with Rogerian doctrine of client-centred casework and is particularly informed by the concept of unconditional positive regard. Rather than demonise parents and overemphasise their shortcomings, including their inadequacies and poor parenting skills, there is instead an attempt to empower by being non-judgemental. The assumption that governs this approach is that with adequate support, a non-judgemental attitude towards the parents and focus on the positives (however little or inconsequential it may appear to those outside the worker – service user relationship) then poor and inadequate parents could be transformed into caring, non-mistreating, good enough parents.

The difficulty with the rule of optimism, as it is currently applied, is that it over-emphasises the caring aspects of social work practice and ignores the control elements. It is an approach that shies away from acknowledging both the positional power of practitioners as well as their legal powers. The approach also assumes a great deal about parental capacity and capability. It expects very little in terms of reciprocity and sees positives where there are none or where there is very little evidence to support such a positive view.

It is important to acknowledge that the rule of optimism was originally perceived as a negative concept. As previously mentioned Dingwall, Eeklaar and Murray (1983) found that practitioners were failing to properly identify the mistreatment of children by their parents and that they overcompensated for inadequate or poor parenting. Blom-Cooper's observation (1985) building on the findings of Dingwall, Eeklaar and Murray, is instructive as he rightly identified two key influential ideas that skew practitioners' perspectives and, as a result, affect their judgement. First he highlighted cultural relativism. Cultural relativism is firmly anchored within the post modern discourse and attempts to redraw the socio-cultural landscape by challenging the way culture is perceived. It encourages diversity within plurality and highlights the way culture reproduces itself through social and interpersonal relations. It exposes the ways in which culture pervades all aspects of the being and how, if left unchecked, promotes the interests and aspirations of the dominant section of society. Cultural relativism questions the universal applicability of 'a' culture and instead posits the notion of fragmentation, fluidity, particularity and culture *in the making*. For cultural relativists it is all about, and in, the narratives. In this world view what constitute appropriate child rearing practices, bad behaviour, and inappropriate attitude in one culture should not be transposed onto another. In other words people's attitude, actions and practices would need to be judged within their cultural background. So instead of being judged by the norms, values, mores and expectations of the society in which they reside the starting point would effectively be their particular familial cultural background. So as Dingwall, Eeklaar and Murray discovered rather than see the mistreatment of children (within this particular society) as inadequate and unacceptable a cultural relativistic perspective would seek to place such behaviour and practices within some kind of understandable relative cultural context. Thus, in such instances, the empathy lies not necessarily with the child but with the neglectful and mistreating parents. The behaviour and attitude of the parent is contextualised and the cultural environment which deems such behaviours and practices acceptable is afforded undue consideration. The second observation by Blom-Cooper relates to the presumption that purely by having a child parents are imbued with instinctive and natural love for their children.

In response to Dingwall, Eeklaar and Murray observations about the level of empathy shown to the mistreating and abusing parents, I would argue that it should always be the case that practitioners take account of the totality of the children's background (including their circumstances, familial and cultural backgrounds) but this should not be at the expense of focusing on what is happening to the child. Empathy is about vicariously entering into the world of the 'other' as a way of understanding their perception and their experience. In my view it is a highly sophisticated tool that allows practitioners to develop a deeper level of understanding of the life world of the 'other'. However as Cree and Myers (2008: 67) cautioned, a practitioner should demonstrate empathy:

> . . . *without becoming enmeshed in the feelings. There is a balancing act to be made in demonstrating that the social worker has truly understood the other's feelings while maintain the distance to be helpful in providing the conditions for growth.*

While practitioners are right to take account of the children's familial background, including their racial, class, culture, and ethnic origin and their religious affiliations (in fact the need to consider these factors are entrenched in child care legislation) these should not be considered outside the context of the society in which they live. Treating a child and their family as if they are immune from the cultural norms, values and mores of society in which they live is both reductive and tantamount to entrenching and reinforcing their exclusion and marginalisation from mainstream society.

In relation to Blom-Cooper's second observation, regarding the presumption as to the nature of the relationship and feelings shown towards the child by the parent, practitioners' experiences could not be clearer on this point. While indeed it may be the case that there is some kind of instinctive and natural love between children and their parents, there is enough evidence from practitioners' own experiences of working with children and their families to suggests that this is not the case in all instances, (see Chapter 4 above by Stroud). In some families, far from the parents emitting love, nurturing intents, safety, comfort and parental instincts, the child or children are more likely to face hostility, brutality, abuse and unimaginable sufferings. It could be suggested that it would be a dereliction of duty for a social work practitioner to believe that in all cases parents, irrespective of their capacity and ability, have positive feelings towards their children and are instinctively able to provide the appropriate nurturing environment for their children to thrive.

Reformulating the rule of optimism

The two elements identified by Blom-Cooper are, in my view, instrumental in the misapplication of the rule of optimism. There is no doubt that the rule of optimism concept does exist and is much in evidence in practice. However rather than ignore it, or attempt to dislodge it from practitioners' consciousness, I believe it needs to be reformulated and refocused differently. It is my contentions that, while the underlying principle of the concept is an important element in nurturing and maintaining service user – worker relationship, it should be read as part of an approach rather than an end in itself. The assumptions underlying the rule of optimism should be commended as it is borne of the desire to empower rather than vilify parents or carers. As previously mentioned, its aim is not to demonise but to instil confidence in parents in order to encourage them to remain *in control*. Practitioners are reluctant to be identified as mere agents of the state whose focus is to exercise their powers by removing children from their parents or carers. Despite the pressure to the contrary practitioners are still interested in holding on to some of the core values of practice – that is to be empathetic, build and maintain service user-worker relationships and practice in a way that is non-discriminatory and non-judgemental. They recognise the impact of poverty on people's lives, the disadvantages that lack of employment brings and the limited opportunities available for those marginalised from society. Practitioners are sensitive to the way that problems the children's parents have to endure can spiral out of control as a result of their situation and circumstance. In this instance the knowledge and understanding that practitioners' possess about the social realities of the children and families they are working with means they are prone to giving parents the benefit of doubt with regards to their behaviour, actions and attitude towards their children. To some extent practitioners' over-identification with the children's parents is understandable even if it is not acceptable. As Arnold (2009) observed, it is not surprising that a social worker would become so close to the family they are working with that they lose their perspective. For Arnold their action, or more appropriately reaction, is not dissimilar to the Stockholm syndrome phenomenon. In this case it is about the nature of the relationship that has developed; the familiarity and closeness fostered; the empathy (indeed sympathy) and the emotional attachment formed over the period of working with the children and their families. In essence, it is possible to provide a rational for the practitioners' approach and the driving force behind their actions. The difficulty is that the rule of optimism, as it is currently adopted, may put the professional judgement of the practitioner in doubt and places the children at risk. The attempt to 'see the good' in people and offer a positive reframing of their day to day lives is commendable however, practitioners have to be on high alert regarding the dangers inherent in the rule of optimism. Thinking about safeguarding and attempting to protect children from harm through the use of legal powers is not necessarily incompatible with working within the rule of optimism framework. In other words it is possible to maintain the (care) positive aspects of the relationship while at the same time being prepared to initiate the necessary procedures (control) required to protect. The skill lies in being able to apply the positive aspects of the rule of optimism while ensuring that the needs, safety and general wellbeing of the children concerned are adequately met.

Minimising risk

Social work with children and families, as previously mentioned, is a complex area of practice that is fraught with difficulties and uncertainties. Whilst the role and responsibilities of practitioners are relatively clear developing sustainable relationships and a working understanding with families is not always easy. Work with children and their families involve practitioners being locked into the world of risk management and all the problems that it entails. In order to avoid the pitfalls of the rule of optimism as identified by Dingwall, Eeklaar and Murray, (1983), practitioners have to be more circumspect, they have to trust their powers of observation, be more challenging and have a higher expectation of parents and carers. Social work training rightly places a great emphasis on assessment which is viewed as the starting point from which everything else flows. Middleton (1997: 5) observed that assessment:

In the social welfare context, it is a basis for planning what needs to be done to maintain or improve a person's situation ... Assessment involves gathering and interpreting information in order to understand a person' and their circumstances; the desirability and feasibility of change and the services and resources which are necessary to affect it. It involves making judgement based on information.

Goodyer (2008) accepted Middleton's underlying premise and further asserted that:

Given the multiplicity of assessment types, the process and skills needed for effective assessment must be varied. The process of evidence based practice is broadly similar to that of research; outline what you are aiming to do, gather existing information, identify new information that will be required, analyse the information and summarise which you have discovered. From an evidence-based model of social work, good assessments are largely seen as those which use multiple sources of information, not relying on one source.

Goodyer, 2008: 98

She also makes clear that:

Professional social work judgements should be based on data integrated from varied methods of assessment, ideally from different assessors, on different occasions in different locations and with varying respondents. Thus, a clearer assessment of a child in need can be made by using records of two different social workers, visiting the family home not just in the daytime, when only one parent may be present, but at different times, also seeing the target child at school, alone, and with siblings. This is likely to offer a relatively broad evidence-base, particularly if parent's views and those of other professionals such as health visitors and teachers are also included.

ibid.

Finally she said;

A social work assessment that was merely based on several home visits, by the same worker at the same time of day is likely to produce a narrower, if deeper, perspective. That type of knowledge-base for an assessment is more typical of a traditional psycho-social assessment.

ibid.

Although Middleton (1997) and Goodyer (2008) placed more emphasis on different aspects of assessment, what unites them is their acknowledgment that assessment is a crucial starting point to any intervention. In my view, what Middleton and Goodyer are encouraging is that greater attention needs to be paid to the way in which information is gathered, analysed and processed.

Staying engaged

As previously mentioned assessment is an important aspect of intervention as it is both the starting point for intervention and its findings provide the raison d'être for the continuing involvement of the practitioner. It is during the ongoing assessment process that the rule of optimism comes to the fore. In situations where practitioners have built a good working relationship with the adults in the family there is potential risk of over familiarity, lack of focus, poor monitoring, uncritical scrutiny of the evidence before them and an over optimistic analysis of the ability and capacity of the adults caring for the child. So instead of a robust and diligent approach, with a critical eye on the situation and condition in which the child is living, there are attempts to assuage and placate the adults in the family. This could lead to little or no challenge of the negative behaviour patterns of the parents and, in some cases, the squalid environment in which the family is living is either ignored or not given due weight. In such cases situations and conditions which would ordinarily be deemed to be unacceptable in any other circumstances are ignored or excused as mere differences of values, mores and life style choices.

In cases where the practitioner is not familiar with the family and has not had time to build a relationship, the problem is further exacerbated. In such instances it is often the case that the family is difficult to engage and they display varying degrees of violence and intimidation towards welfare professionals. Practitioners are often confronted with people who are uncooperative and a great deal of guile is used to distract the practitioner from focusing on the presenting problem and the child. Moreover, great skills are deployed in ensuring that the practitioner never has full access to the children in the family. It is not unusual in such families that the level of aggression and intimidation is so fierce that practitioners are generally reluctant or too frightened to make the necessary home visits or be persistent in making contact with the family. What practitioners need to keep at the forefront of their minds in such instances is that if they are so afraid or intimidated by such families what about the children living in such an environment, what kinds of lives do such children have? It is in these kinds of situation that practitioners need to be more aware of their positional power. Although it is uncomfortable to mention it is nevertheless worthwhile to acknowledge that the whole edifice of social services and social work were created to provide both care *and* control. As a general rule care and control are seen as opposites however, within the context of social work practice they are in fact two aspects of a continuum. In other words they do not cancel each other out nor does the use of one mean that the other is irrelevant and redundant. So, to care may mean having to exercise control and exercising control could also involve a great deal of caring and providing emotional and psychological support.

Conclusion

This chapter has explored the connection between practitioners' reluctance to exert and exercise their legal powers with confidence and their desire to work in a way that is non-judgemental, oppressive or discriminatory. I have tried to argue that the reluctance to utilise their powers is much influenced by a number factors, including the rule of optimism approach. However, it is suggested that the rule of optimism need not necessarily be viewed negatively, and the underlying idea of seeing the positives in people (who have been identified as inadequate, poor parents, irresponsible, incapable of ensuring the health, safety and welfare of their children) is not in itself a bad approach. The difficulty is when, in an effort not to marginalise and reinforce negative attributes, practitioners disconnect themselves from their professional responsibility to safeguard and prevent ill-treatment and abuse. While the aim at all times should be to show respect and professionalism it is important not to lose sight of the fact that social services and social workers are involved with the family because of concerns about the welfare of the child(ren). Paradoxically all the hard of work put into keeping the family together, supporting the parents and accentuating the positives could lead to tragic consequence if the rule of optimism is misapplied.

Social work is about, and has always been about, care and control. While there is a great deal of understanding of what the care element entails, the way power is often viewed and interpreted by practitioners is lineal and one-dimensional.

I believe it is important to recognise that the rule of optimism does sit comfortably within the care and control doctrine and having to exercise power in order to support, protect and safeguard should not be viewed as being incompatible. Taking decisive action against abusive and neglectful parents is not in itself a failure. Practitioners should not be afraid to use the full powers that are vested in them, nor should they allow themselves to be manipulated by those they are trying to help and protect. As already highlighted earlier, the core principles of the rule of optimism are not necessarily negative but they need to be balanced against the harsh reality of the behaviours and attitudes of some the families that are of cause for concern. It is evident that social workers generally attempt to balance the need to be fair, just and anti-discriminatory against the need to act, even when it is not asked for. There will always be tension between building a trusting relationship with a family and acting, when necessary, in a way that undermines and erodes that trust. But this is the nature of the work.

Reference

Arnold, G. (2009) Stressful, Underpaid, and It's Downright Dangerous. *The Times*, 8 May.
Beckett, C. (2009) The Ethics of Control. *Ethics and Social Welfare*, 3: 3, 229–33.

Blom-Cooper, L. (1985) *A Child in Trust: The Report of the Commission of Inquiry into the Circumstances Surrounding The Death of Jasmine Beckford.* London, London, Borough of Brent.

Braye, S. and Preston-Shoot, M. (2009) *Practising Social Work Law.* 3rd edn. Basingstoke: Palgrave Macmillan.

Cree, V. and Myers, S. (2008) *Social Work: Making a Difference.* Bristol, The Policy Press.

Colby, I. (2007) Forward. In Graham, M. (2007) *Black Issues in Social Work and Social Care.* Bristol, Polity Press.

Dingwall, R., Eeklaar, J. and Murray, T. (1983) *The Protection of Children: State Intervention and Family Life.* Oxford, Blackwell.

Goodyer, A. (2008) Assessment in Practice. In Okitikpi, T. and Aymer, C. (2008) *The Art of Social Work Practice.* Lyme Regis, Russell House Publishing.

Horner, N. (2003) *What is Social Work? Context and Perspectives.* Exeter, Learning Matters.

Laming, H. (2009) *The Protection of Children in England: A Progress Report.* London, DCSF.

Mandell, D. (2008) Power, Care and Vulnerability: Considering Use of Self In Child Welfare Work. *Journal of Social Work Practice*, 22: 2, 235–48.

Middleton, L. (1997) *The Art of Assessment.* Birmingham, Venture Press.

O'Brian, C.P. (2003) Resource and Educational Empowerment: A Social Work Paradigm For The Disenfranchised. *Research on Social Work Practice.* 13: 3, 388–99.

Ofsted (2009) *Learning Lessons from Serious Case Reviews: Year 2.* Manchester: Ofsted.

Sheppard, D. (1996) *Learning the Lessons.* 2nd edn. London: Zito Trust.

Smith, R. (2008) *Social Work and Power.* Basingstoke, Palgrave Macmillan.

Tew, J. (2006) Understanding Power and Powerlessness: Towards a Framework for Emancipatory Practice in Social Work. *Journal of Social Work*, 6: 1, 33–51.

CHAPTER 6

Social Work and Social Workers Powers – A Lay Perspective

Sarah Pond

Introduction

The main focus of this book is about social control and children and families social work practise in the 21st century. More specifically it is trying to explore the social work profession's understanding of it's statutory powers and the extent to which they are prepared to use such powers. This chapter explores the perception of social workers and the social work profession from a lay person's point of view. I am particularly keen to consider both how the profession is presented in the press and to offer a general lay perspective of the profession.

As a starting point I must confess that when first asked to write this chapter I was somewhat apprehensive as I found myself having a private battle in my head. I believe that social work is a highly valuable profession and one that contributes to society by supporting those who are most needy. Yet when I discuss future career choices with my children, I hesitate to suggest this as a potential option. Why is that? I can only suppose that press stories have once again heightened the public attention on the entire care sector and shown its failings to extreme and horrifying effect. Would I want my children to be a part of a profession where every case is by its nature a challenging one and if mistakes happen somewhere in the chain, then the consequences are not only dire for the person concerned but the professionals involved are vilified. If I don't want that for my children then how many other people feel similarly? What does that mean for the future of the profession – are the people who choose to follow this career path mad or stupid? Or are there still good people out there who genuinely care about their fellow human beings and want to help however difficult the job may be?

My assumption about social work is that it is a highly pressurised environment where newly qualified staff are not well supported to undertake their role and due to shortages in just about every social work team in the country. I assume that they will always have a workload far in excess of what they can reasonably manage therefore mistakes will happen because vulnerable people will fall through the net. I want my children to make a career choice that will reward them for success; support and promote their continued personal development and leave them with a sense of fulfilment. Whilst deep inside I know there must be huge rewards in social work when it all goes right, the fear of what the personal impact to the social worker is when things go wrong far outweighs the positives in my mind.

What is social work?

I began by thinking about how one would describe not just social work in general but their role, duties, responsibilities and the extent of their powers. In thinking about those who work in the profession I think about people who fundamentally care; who want to do something which will bring benefits to vulnerable people. This then begged the question, who are the vulnerable people? To some extent they could be characterised as families or individuals with various needs, problems or difficulties; (single) parents living in over-crowded properties on low incomes with little social or familial network of support; families where one or more members have a long-term health problem or addiction; elderly people with little or no family support; people with mental health problems; people who have history of drug or alcohol abuse or those who have been convicted of crimes and their families. Some of these people may be described by the general public as undeserving of social work support as oppose to others who may have fallen victim to circumstance beyond their control. However, by and large in my mind, the role of the social worker is varied and may include the provision of practical help; emotional support; general advice and perhaps helping individuals and/or families to regain their strengths and rediscover their coping mechanism.

What do social workers do?

As a lay person it is difficult to get a clear sense of what social workers actually do and it is even more impossible to describe the full extent of their tasks, duties and responsibilities. But according to the Department of Health, (DOH,), social work is described as being both complicated and simple and it involves working with people. More precisely the DoH (2010: 5) explained that:

> Social workers form relationships with people. As adviser, advocate, counsellor or listener, a social worker helps people to live more successfully within their local communities by helping them find solutions to their problems. Social work also involves engaging not only with clients themselves but their families and friends as well as working closely with other organisations including the police, NHS, schools and probation service.

There is a specific status associated with the job title 'social worker'. Social workers are professionally qualified staff that assess the needs of service users and plan the individual packages of care and support that would best provide help and support for people.

This above definition identifies some key phrases that describe a role I would identify as that of a social worker. The fact that it is a people focused role is exactly how I perceive it; in addition there is a strong focus on helping *clients* or service users to find solutions to their problems and supporting them as individuals. The language used suggests a role which is about empowerment; helping people in difficulty to find a way out of those difficulties and it is the social worker who listens to those people and gives them advice and support. I would say these are all the positive aspects of the role of a being social worker that I would easily have identified. But this description on its own is surely looking at the profession through rose-coloured spectacles. There is another, more harder edge side to the role of being a social worker which is about protecting vulnerable people.

There are some significant omissions in the description above, which I think gets to the core of the concern held by a large sector of the general public. While the word 'protection' is evident; the word 'safety' is missing, and the description is focused entirely on helping and supplying service users. This omission could be seen as being of fundamental problem for the profession. In other words has the role of social workers moved so far away from protection, ensuring safety and improving life chances towards a glorified befriending service? Can one person do both, i.e. be supportive and give help where needed and act as an advocate but still make hard, tough decisions when required to ensure protection of the most vulnerable? If there is an expectation that the same person can do both, and I believe there is, then the DoH description above does not make that clear enough. I therefore wondered whether there is any part of the social worker's assessment, induction or training process that is more direct about the harder-edged aspects of the role. As the primary aim is to keep people safe from harm then I would have expected greater emphasis on ensuring that practitioners are aware of their powers. So why does the issue of power and use of draconian powers (when necessary) feature in the description offered by the Department of Health? Is their description of the role misleading to potential social workers about the reality of the issues they will have to face? Is that a wise stance for them to take?

Reading the General Social Care Council's (GSCC, 2008) professional standards and what is expected of social workers I was in part reassured but also somewhat disturbed by what I found. Looking through the Council's Code of Practice, the word 'respect' comes up eight times; the word 'protect' comes up five times but the context in which these terms are used relates largely to the protection of the rights and views of service users and not about protecting vulnerable people and there is little reference to the safeguarding role. The Code of Practice (2008: 13) contains the following, 'As a social care worker, you must respect the rights of service users while seeking to ensure that their behaviour does not harm themselves or other people'. This is a clear reference to social workers having a key role in protecting others who may come to harm but it is buried amongst multiple references to support and respecting the rights of the client. I therefore feel there is a fundamental difficulty for social workers in that this code places the emphasis so heavily upon the role of protecting the rights and decisions of the service users that the aspect of the role that relates to protection is very much played down and does not feature so prominently.

Is it this that prompts the view held by a section of society that social workers are left-wing do-gooders who just want to be friends and cannot see wrong in anyone? Does the Code of Practice fairly acknowledge the complexity and responsibility that social workers are working with? Is this code doing an injustice to the profession? I wonder.

I feel frustrated with the language used in the regulation of social work which leads me to an understanding of the indignation felt by a large proportion of the general public. I hope drawing attention to these deficits may help those in the profession to see why the wider public may hold such negative views about social workers and their ineffectiveness. The emphasis for the role of the social worker is very definitely focused upon the service user and having respect for them and their rights. I feel however, that there is a potential for conflict within the role that means the social worker has a responsibility for protecting vulnerable people who may be in the care of people that are causing them harm but who themselves are clients or service users. This potential difficulty in role definition pushes me towards the view that is held by a section of the general public that social workers are more concerned with being friends with and respecting the rights of the 'user' than they are with identifying vulnerable people who are at risk. I looked again at the regulation to see where the absolute requirements for social workers are defined.

For example, Page 6 of the Code of Practice includes the following bullet points under the heading *Social Care Workers must . . .*

- *Protect the rights and promote the interests of service users and carers.*
- *Strive to establish and maintain the trust and confidence of service users and carers.*
- *Promote the independence of service users while protecting them as far as possible from danger or harm.*
- *Respect the rights of service users whilst seeking to ensure that their behaviour does not harm themselves or other people.*
- *Uphold public trust and confidence in social care services.*
- *Be accountable for the quality of their work and take responsibility for maintaining and improving their knowledge and skills.*

My understanding of this list as a lay person is that these are the absolutes, the non-negotiable elements of the role. Reading through them, the first three in my interpretation focus upon protecting the interests and rights of service users, I have no difficulty with that as one important and fundamental aspect of the role, but half of the 'must do's' are focused upon that support to the service user. The fourth point has an absolute in 'respect the rights . . .' and a phrase which to my mind is less absolute, 'whilst seeking to ensure . . .' this second part of the bullet point suggests that is a secondary factor – the word 'seek' means 'to try to find or obtain' (Oxford English Dictionary, 2007) therefore it is not as absolute as the straight 'you must . . . respect'. I interpret that to mean that ensuring harm does not come to others is of secondary consideration after the rights of the service user have been respected. That surely cannot be what was intended when the code was developed?

As a lay person I would have assumed that there would have been a bullet point which would have said something like 'you must ensure the behaviour of your client does not cause harm to others' and 'you must report immediately should you have concerns that there is potential for your client to cause harm to themselves or others'. Although it could be argued that these expectations are implied and are therefore embedded as part of the general duties. However, in my view, I think they need to be made more explicit from a national level in order to ensure a consistent standard throughout the country.

The word 'risk' appears in the GSCC Code of Practice 10 times; significantly on page 14 the following statement appears, 'Following risk assessment policies and procedures to assess whether the behaviour of service users presents a risk of harm to themselves or others'. This makes a clear statement that risk assessment policies must be in place and must be followed by social workers. Risk assessment policies are set at a local level. Given that this is such a critical part of the protection of vulnerable people, I wonder if this should be prescribed from a national level in order to ensure a consistent standard throughout the country.

Safeguarding and children and families social work

The Department for Children, Schools and Families (DCSF, 2010) published a document entitled *Working Together to Safeguard Children: A guide to inter-agency working to safeguard and promote the welfare of children.* This document followed a public consultation which ended in February 2010 and includes a number of recommendations from Lord Laming's reports. Since the cases of Victoria Climbie, Baby Peter and others have hit the public consciousness there has been a flurry of activity in terms of new legislation and guidance around Children's services. There seems to be a whole new 'industry' involved in the identification and protection of vulnerable children. So can we all sit back now in the knowledge that such tragedies cannot arise in the future? I would suggest there is cause for some optimism and hope but I fear that the root of the problem has yet to be properly addressed.

The document states that; 'Only in exceptional cases should there be compulsory intervention in family life – for example, where this is necessary to safeguard a child from significant harm' (DCSF 2010: 30). It seems to me that this is a case of stating the obvious but is interesting that this point needs stating. There is again a strong focus upon working with families. Most people would accept the premise that where they are in a safe environment then children should, as best as possible, be supported within their family. But I think the general public knows and accepts, indeed wants to see the evidence that professionals will act in situations where the child's home environment is the unsafe option and take any action necessary for the welfare and protection of the child.

The document acknowledges what must be the dilemma that social workers have to face on a regular basis; 'Judgments on how best to intervene . . . entail an element of risk . . . leaving a child for too long in a dangerous situation or of removing a child unnecessarily . . . (ibid.). These are the risks that I believe the public expects social workers to be able to handle and manage and make decisions based on assessment of those risks. Whilst I would be very concerned about over-zealous 'bureaucrats' wrongly removing children from safe family homes; if the risk of leaving them means they could come to serious harm or even die, then there has to be a balance towards offering the child protection from such an environment.

I wonder if there are alternatives, perhaps a break for both parent and child may in itself be sufficient to bring about the necessary changes for the child to be able to return home safely. Should a child be removed from their home, regular and frequent assessment should be undertaken so that support can be given to the family to be able to provide the child a safe home in the future, albeit with support. I believe the vast majority of the public would believe this to be a critical and essential part of the role of the social worker.

A strong feature of this document is upon 'child-centred' care, 'The significance of seeing and observing the child cannot be overstated. The child should be spoken and listened to, and their wishes and feelings ascertained, taken into account (having regard to their age and understanding) and recorded . . . Some of the worst failures of the system have occurred when professionals have lost sight of the child and concentrated instead on their relationship with the adults' (DCSF, 2010: 133). This sentence surprised me in some respects – is this the key component that has been missing from guidance and codes of conduct thus far? As a lay person, I perhaps naively assumed that where a child was the subject of social work intervention or assessment they would be spoken to by the lead worker in order to find out the problem. It seems an obvious point to make but how else could one possibly begin to understand if there is a real risk of harm or abuse without seeing or talking to the child concerned? The final sentence sums up for me what is potentially the problem not only in 'the worst failures' but in the way social work has evolved in recent years – befriending and working with the parent but without offering that same regard and respect to the child. Of course, working with parents has to be a key part of any social workers role in protecting children at risk, but the first priority is the child and as such the child should have a right and an entitlement to speak for themselves. If this document is seeking to address this gap then it does pick the issue up, but as this comment is on page 133 of a 394 page document how can the public be sure these key changes in emphasis are being picked up by those who need to implement the change?

In many ways a detailed report such as this does deal with the issues that are of concern but it also raises a lot more questions. For example are workers trained to relate to, work with and understand children and parents? Will the Code of Practice be amended to take account for these changes? With the shortage in qualified social workers, how will local authorities meet the requirements specified in the guidance? Will all the time spent in case conferences, presenting reports to safeguarding Boards and reporting to Children's trusts add further delays to a system that is being changed in order to allow more rapid response? Are there sufficient resources within local government to support the structure? The news is full of stories of local government budgets being under extreme pressure – what will have to be forsaken in order to support the structure? Will other areas of social care become over-shadowed and depleted of resources in order to meet these standards? Whenever a serious problem is highlighted and catches the attention of the public, as these issues have, it is generally followed up with a flurry of activity and multiple changes in regulation, operation and reporting but generally the urgency of being seen to do something (however irrelevant) is often preferred to looking seriously at the underlying issues involved.

Social workers and their powers

I have always assumed that social workers, as well as working closely with families in difficulty, had a number of powers including removing children from their home environment when their well-being is a risk. From previous experience, I also understand that they have a role in mental health assessment. Along with those powers, I had a vague notion that social workers have powers to bring in support and help where and when they are needed. Those thoughts are a little mixed up and unclear but I was content in my view that social workers had a number of powers that could be utilised as required. However, in preparing this chapter, it was with some surprise that I found that the most serious powers that I had associated with those of a social worker actually have to be endorsed by the courts or executed by the police. For example with *Child Assessment Order* the social worker must go through the family court and make application for an Assessment order. Only once that order has been granted can such an assessment be undertaken.

Again the *Emergency Protection Order* must be applied for through the court and will only be granted if the court believes that a child is likely to suffer significant harm. The fact that the court has a role in granting this order should therefore offer a safeguard. Similarly for *Power to enter premises* the social worker must call the police if they suspect a child is in immediate danger – they cannot enter a home or apply for a warrant. Even in extreme emergency, it is the police who have the power to enter a property (under a *Police Protection Order*).

The *Child Protection Conference* is a multi-agency affair with meetings held on behalf of the Local Safeguarding Children Board (LSCB) to decide if a child is at risk of significant harm and if so recommend a child protection plan (Wiltshire Local Safeguarding Board, 2010). Once again, this is not a decision taken by social workers alone, the emphasis is very much on a multi-agency approach.

This discovery led me to ponder a different area which had not really occurred to me before: why is it that the social worker is vilified when these orders have to pass through the rigour of the family court system? Surely that process offers an assurance and an additional safety net or security blanket that should ensure judgements made have a sound basis and have been scrutinised? Or are the courts simply 'rubber-stamping' recommendations made by social workers without properly making their own assessment about the merits of the case?

This whole area has caused me to think again about the general perception that social workers possess legal powers that enables them to disrupt families' lives and remove children with no recourse to any other authority. This knowledge has highlighted a further set of issues.

1. If it is the courts that have the authority to approve these applications, what evidence are they seeking to enable them to make a judgement?
2. If the police can take emergency action under a police protection order, what evidence do they seek to enable them to make that judgement?
3. How many applications are rejected? Given that for many of these orders, there is a very tight turnaround time set, is it possible for courts to be robust in making their judgement?
4. If courts are able to make robust judgements then why is it that the social worker takes the can for decisions that are deemed to be wrong, when it is the court that has granted the order?
5. And finally if the courts cannot make robust judgements in the timeframe laid down then what is the point?

Would it not be better to be open and state that courts are really only rubber-stamping these applications and instead give the total responsibility over to social workers so that they can make decisions to carry out these orders but in the knowledge that they can and will be scrutinised for the robustness of their evidence. In some ways having the court system involved in this process offers the social worker a 'second opinion', knowing that the court has the power to refuse it. I could understand a scenario where a social worker might feel that a case is worth putting before a neutral, independent body to seek their judgement. In my view, this again suggests a system that seems flawed. Social workers are being asked to make serious recommendations to a court; the court can take a different view but in the eyes of the public it is the social worker who is accountable not the court, yet the social worker does not have ultimate accountability. I begin to wonder how this system actually succeeds at all – the odds seem stacked against it.

Is it right that hearings in family courts are conducted in private?

In the course of my reading, another key concern emerged. The family courts, by their very nature, are dealing with sensitive individual issues relating to children, are conducted in private. As a result of intense pressure some of the confidentiality restrictions were lifted in April 2009 and the press is now able to attend family court hearings, albeit with tight restrictions and a requirement that consent must be obtained from the court to print anything about the case. However, there remains a lobby for opening up family courts further. Those in favour suggest that the screen of confidentiality is being used by social workers to portray exaggerated or untrue allegations against parents or carers. The confidential nature of the hearing means that only those present can challenge such allegations and of course they are the very people against whom the allegations are made.

I can see to some extent the argument made both for and against opening up the family court system. From the limited published data available, children themselves have expressed concerns that if the family courts are opened up, then their confidentiality would be compromised. Given that family courts must primarily have the interests of children at heart then this view has to be respected. However, as it has been argued, there does seem to be a need for some kind of accountability which is missing from the system at present. Of course, the views of children must be highly regarded but it seems this needs to be balanced against instances whereby parents are accused of varying degree of failures or abuse and feel they are locked into a closed system that is unfairly set against them. It seems an obvious point to make, but worth making in any case, but it would be fairer and just to devise a system that would allow accused parents/cares to challenge accusations against them and given the opportunity to express their views and produce any experts or witnesses in support of their case. Despite its shortcomings, one of the strengths of the British legal system is its ability to cope with conflicting evidence and reaching a judgment.

Social workers as 'enthusiastic removers of children'

In researching for this chapter it became clear that there is a contradiction in the public perceptions of social workers reaction towards children at risk. On the one hand there is a strongly held view that social workers are 'lightweight' professionals who miss abused children. On the other hand there is another strongly-held and equally concerning view that social workers are arrogant, risk-averse individuals who would take a child away from its family rather than work to keep the child safe at home. This is part of the muddled environment within which social workers operate.

In April 2010, Lord Justice Wall was appointed president of the Family Division of the High Court. He is quoted by Bennett (2010) as saying that; 'social workers need to be aware that the public perception is that they are enthusiastic removers of children from their parents'. He is further quoted as saying; 'We may have gone too far in suspecting abuse'. It is my belief that this view is not the public perception at the present time. I believe there is a greater public perception that social workers do **not** enthusiastically remove children enough – even from abusive households. However, the view expressed by Lord Justice Wall is shared by a particular section of the community. Whilst I do not take the same view, there is sufficient 'noise' on forums, blogs etc on the internet to suggest that a significant number of people believe this to be true. In addition there are organisations established to support those who are victims of this risk-averse side of social workers; these include FASSIT (Families and Social Services Information Team) and no2abuse, amongst others. Within their web-sites are tales of families who have lost children to forced adoption. It is in relation to two of these cases that Lord Justice Walls' comments were made.

Published data suggests that the numbers of children being taken away from their families has been increasing over a number of years and the numbers further increased by 40 per cent in the year following the trial of Baby Peter's parents. What this means is that we have a system which misses cases of terrible abuse of some children alongside one in which other children are being taken, perhaps wrongly, from families with safe home environments. In my view a system which allows both of these extreme positions is a system in trouble. If the problem was that there were many children taken into care but very few tragedies, then it could be justified. Conversely, if very few children were taken away from their families but child death rates from abuse were high, again this would be understandable. It is important to note that I'm not saying that either position would be acceptable but in order to change those statistics, it would simply mean that a different approach to risk was needed. However, we have, it seems, these two extremes positions side by side. To me, as an ordinary but interested individual, that suggests social workers may be working within a fundamentally flawed system. Perhaps the two extremes suggest different attitudes to risk in different local authorities – after all, thresholds are set as part of the local strategy.

Conclusion

This has been an interesting period of exploration for me having discovered much that I didn't know. Social workers do not, on the face of it, have the powers I thought they had and found that there are some diametrically opposing views about whether social workers are too friendly with clients or are too suspicious of parents. As a lay person I continue to feel there is a real difficulty for those in the profession; I feel that the Code of Practice places a heavy emphasis upon supporting and respecting the views of clients without sufficiently acknowledging the protection role which social workers also carry. I feel there are likely to be many occasions where a social worker would be placed in a 'no win' situation. In my view there is a need for some fundamental change which would allow social workers to continue to support vulnerable families but which similarly supports them to make hard, tough decisions where those families are at risk of causing harm.

The views expressed are those which I hold now on the basis of what I have read and considered. I have not had any informed discussion with those who carry out a hands on role in social care because I really wanted to offer a perspective to the profession of what a partially informed lay person may see as the world of the social worker. I hope this is useful and informative. It is not intended to be another attempt to 'beat up' the social worker; I really do admire those who work with such dedication in such very difficult circumstances. It might be helpful to just get an idea of why those of us outside the profession hold the views that are expressed in the media or across the internet; I hope this is of some benefit in that regard.

What about my view of social work as a career choice for my children? I have to say that whilst I remain ignorant of much of the detail around the role, I do feel having explored the matter in some detail I now have a slightly more informed view about social work and social workers. Whilst supporting my children in any profession they decide to pursue, social work is, without doubt, a tough profession. I continue to believe that there is a very real risk for those working in the social work profession of being 'damned if you do and damned if you don't' and I feel the current system has encouraged this approach. For me, there needs to be some serious review of the existing roles and responsibilities of social workers. There is scope for consideration of a division of responsibility between a family support social worker and a family assessment social worker for want of a better distinction. I feel such a separation of those duties between professionals would remove the conflict within the role of one person potentially being both the defence and the prosecution.

If my children do consider social work as a career, I would not say don't do it but I would strongly advise them to do as much homework as they could before embarking on such a career. I would advise they spend time in a social work team; to do some voluntary work in a related area, to speak to social workers about their work and how they cope with the daily difficulties, dilemmas and problems they encounter in their work. In my view social work is a vitally important role and one which should be held in much higher esteem by the general public akin to the medical or nursing professions. I hope the result of the heightened media attention is that it leads to increased resources and changes in attitude towards the profession. There needs to be more recognition of the dedication and professionalism of many social workers.

References

Bennett, R. (13.4.10) We May Have Gone Too Far in Suspecting Abuse. *Times on-line* Available at: http://business.timesonline.co.uk/tol/business/law/article7095772.ece (Accessed 26.4.10)

DfCSF (2010) *Working Together to Safeguard Children: A Guide to Inter-Agency Working to Safeguard and Promote The Welfare of Children.* London, HMSO.

DoH (2010) *What is Social Work? The Role.* Available at http://www.socialworkcareers.co.uk/what/index.asp (accessed 10.1.10)

FASSIT – www.fassit.co.uk

General Social Care Council (2008) *Codes of Practice for Social Care Workers.* London, GSCC.

no2abuse – www.no2abuse.com

Oxford English Dictionary On-line (2007) Oxford University Press, 2007 Available at: http://www.askoxford.com/concise_oed/seek?view = uk (Accessed 24.4.10)

Wiltshire Local Safeguarding Board *Child Protection Conferences: A Guide for Families* Available at http://www.wiltshirelscb.org/material/child-protect-conference.pdf (accessed on 24.4.10)

CHAPTER 7

The Use of Power in Social Work Practice

Amanda Thorpe

Introduction

This chapter aims to examine notions of power, how social work practitioners use power in practice, the drivers and constraints involved in using the range of powers available, and the ways in which statutory power may be used both to promote and undermine ethical practice. Ideas of managerialism, deprofessionalisation, reflexivity and reflective practice are considered, as is the social worker's understanding and application of the legal rules. Recommendations are made to help ensure that practitioners use, as appropriate, the full extent of their statutory and professional powers to promote safe, ethical and anti-oppressive practice. According to Smith (2008):

> *Power dynamics in social work depend on the complex interplay between . . . different aspects of the practitioner's identity, standing and imputed authority, and those with whom the practitioner is interacting, notably service users, as well as those who may play a part in influencing interventions.*

Smith, 2008: 3

In order to understand how practitioners use power, it is important to consider the nature and scope of power and the different dimensions of power which practitioners have at their disposal. Power is, itself a contested concept, (Lukes, 2005; Hugman, 1991; Tew, 2002, 2006; Smith, 2008) and the detailed examination of which is beyond the scope of this chapter. The extent to which social work practitioners engage with the various dimensions of power, however, and their ability to use this effectively in their practice will be discussed. Power is frequently used in the sense of 'power over', that is the ability to exert force, be it physical, intellectual or structural, but also in the sense of 'power to', an ability to make something happen. Tew (2006) also adds the notion of 'power together', drawing from feminist psychology, as a more egalitarian and empowering concept.

Social workers need to be able to engage with a range of different conceptions of power and to understand the differences and know what conception of power they are using at any point, and for what purpose. So to use Tew's (2006) notions of power, social work practitioners will at various times be using many dimensions of power in their practice. For example:

- *Power to* conduct an investigation.
- *Power together* – to work in partnership to re-establish safety/equilibrium.
- *Power over* – to impose requirements to do/not do, e.g. remove a child.

Alongside these notions of power is the requirement to use power consciously and responsibly. Social work practice and decision making is governed by the principles of administrative law and as Welbourne notes, 'Social Workers need to be held accountable because they exercise power in a position of responsibility and authority'', (Welbourne, in Long, et al., 2010: 106).

In order to be able to exercise power effectively and in an anti-oppressive manner, social workers also need to understand the various pressures and multiple accountabilities that they have to negotiate in practice. Eby (in Brechin et al., 2000) refers to the ways in which the practitioner is shaped by the range of pressures on them and how they change shape in response to the particular dominant pressure at any one time. The practitioner in this analogy is referred to as a single cell organism operating in an environment of complexity, expected to adapt and respond as pressures shift and change. This model underlines therefore the importance of drawing on multiple perspectives in practice in order to understand the different ways in which a single event or situation might be understood by the range of players involved. For example, the practitioner's perspective needs to be set alongside the manager's and service user's perspective in order to understand how the multiple dimensions of a case add to or reduce the understanding of risk. If one perspective is allowed to dominate then the risk is of, at best, an inaccurate assessment and at worst the missing of important indicators which might require the use of legal powers.

From the experience of working with social work students and post-qualifying practitioners in an educational context it is clear that practitioners, and those about to enter the profession, often see power in a simplistic and one-dimensional way. Lukes (2005: 29) describes the one-dimensional view of power as focusing on 'behaviour, decision making, (key) issues, observable (overt) conflict and (subjective) interests'. In his analysis of power he observes that 'power is . . . ineradicably value dependent', but further notes that the value assumptions underpinning the understanding and application of power are often unacknowledged. One of the critiques of social work that will be explored later in this chapter is that of the de-professionalisation of social work practice. It might be argued that the move to a more vocational, rather than professional, framework of initial qualifying education has led students, and the practitioners they become, to take a somewhat simplistic view of power, empowerment, oppression and anti-oppressive practice, rather than engaging in the more intellectually challenging understanding of power as a contested concept within which managers, practitioners and service users embody multiple power relationships. Westwood (2002) describes a conception of power needing to take 'a 'quantum' approach, based not on either/or dichotomies which oversimplify complex social realities, but rather on both/ and formulations which seek to capture the diversity, complexity and depth of the social world', (Westwood, 2002, cited in Thompson, 2003: 50). By engaging with the interconnec-tedness of power dynamics in the context of both individual and professional power, practitioners may be better able explicitly to engage with the multi-dimensional relationship of power, rather than the binary modes of powerful v powerless, oppressive v oppressed.

Social work practitioners themselves, however, often report feeling 'powerless' (Jones, 2001; Smith, 2008) either in the face of protracted and complex practice situations, by the restricted resources available to them to effect change, or by their role in the organisation. There is however a lack of congruence between social workers' feelings of powerlessness and service users' perceptions of social workers as being 'powerful'; able to use legal and positional power for or against them. As Smith (2008: 17) notes, social workers are 'at one and the same time, acutely aware of their own relative powerlessness in an organisational and structural sense, and yet concerned as to how to manage their own authority over service users'. In discussing this theme with a group of Post-Qualifying students it was clear that, in their view, service users would always see the social worker's power as 'draconian' and suggested that 'as social workers, maybe we don't put in the building blocks of relationship building because we know we may have to draw back and use those statutory and "draconian" powers'. It is perhaps then because of this disconnection between practitioners' perceptions of their own power and service users' position of relative powerlessness that the tension in using statutory powers is created. As one social worker asked:

Should we be going into families initially stating our powers and the possible conse-quences, rather than the 'softly, softly' voluntary family support and then moving to legal powers when this fails?

Power and reflexivity

Mandell (2008) explores the concept of 'use of self' in relation to child welfare work, focusing specifically on the power dimensions of the worker-service user relationship. She argues that the worker's social location and identity impacts on their understanding and use of power in the professional relationship. Similarly Smith (2008) as noted earlier, acknowledges that there is a complex inter-relationship between the practitioner's role, identity and power, and those with whom they interact, whether service users or other professionals. Perceptions of power therefore may be linked in the service user's mind to personal characteristics such as race, age, gender, etc. as well as role and professional identity. Mandell further notes that, 'anti-oppressive practice requires not only cultural sensitivity but an accompanying commitment to recognising and addressing power imbalances arising from different social locations', (Mandell, 2008: 240).

It is therefore important also to look at the notion of reflexivity as well as the requirements for reflective practice, if practitioners are effectively to both understand and use their powers. In essence:

Power cannot be removed from the encounter between worker and service user, no matter how kind, self-aware or careful the worker may be . . . workers have an obligation to engage in critical self-reflection on all these aspects of self and other and agencies are obligated to enable and support this activity.

Mandell, 2008: 244–5

The difficult decisions required by the child protection and child welfare mandate must therefore take into account reflexively, dimensions of power and privilege, identity and social location and knowledge drawn from theory and research and practice experience. The critically reflective practitioner will need therefore to develop a matrix within which their own privilege, sense of self, knowledge and experience are set in the context of explicit power relations and notions of ethical and anti-oppressive practice. The risk for front-line practitioners is that the disjunction between their sense of what they want and need to do, that is their powers, with what they feel able to do, their sense of powerlessness, results in an emotional detachment from the service user as a means of self-protection, (Mandell, 2008). The result of such detachment and consequent de-personalisation of the service user is to render collaborative working and a sense of 'power together', (Tew, 2006), with those with whom they are working, almost impossible.

One of the reasons cited for practitioners feeling powerless is their position in large bureaucratic organisations. Statutory social work takes place most of the time within large local government departments who have complex structures of management and accountability and are linked to central government and policy drivers. Within this structure, the individual front line social worker can feel like a very small cog in a very large wheel. The advance of 'managerialism' since the 1980s (Banks, 2004; Dickens, 2008; Lymbery, 1998; Smith, 2008; Thompson, 2003, 2010) has contributed to the regulation, control and oversight of what the individual social worker does. Similarly the key drivers are targets, deadlines and bureaucracy rather than professional processes. As Thompson (2010: 51) notes

'. . . the development of managerialism has had major implications and consequences in terms of a reduction in professional confidence and pride, producing feelings of being de-skilled and devalued'.

Fook and Gardner (2007) identify four main categories of organisational response to dealing with risk, uncertainty and complexity. These are:

1. 'working to rules and procedures', for example the increasing burden of policies and guidelines in response to public enquiries, (Cleveland, 1988; Victoria Climbié, 2003; Baby Peter, 2009).
2. 'generating paperwork', with the participants in Fook and Gardner's research identifying a sense of the priority in practice being the completion of the paperwork, rather than focusing on service users.
3. they identify the ways in which organisations respond by breaking down the tasks into clearly defined and 'manageable' areas. This can be seen at both the macro and micro levels with increasing separation between adult and children's services at both governmental and organisational level. The allocation of aspects of on-going case work to unqualified workers in the form of face to face work with children, with the intention of freeing up the qualified worker to focus on the 'professional task' is such an example. This separation, at whatever level, reduces the ability of the practitioner to take a holistic approach which takes into account the multiple dimensions of a situation. Conversations with service users clearly identify the need for work across these artificial and bureaucratic boundaries, to paraphrase the words of a disabled parent, 'it may have escaped the government's attention but my needs and those of my child are inextricably linked'.
4. Finally, Fook and Gardner identify a 'focus on outcomes', or a quantitative rather than qualitative approach to measuring performance, noting that it is easier to measure the number of visits or timescales within which work is completed than the less tangible quality of the relationship between social worker and family. They note this as a concern generated by the 'tension between value-based professional practice and economically and technically focused organisations' (Fook and Gardner, 2007: 9).

The impact of managerialism on social workers use of power

Writing about issues of autonomy and managerialism in respect of adult services and community care, Lymbery links the change in the social worker's role to that of 'care manager' with concerns about de-professionalisation. He argues that the impact of an increased emphasis on procedural and managerial requirements has been to 'locate an increasing control of practice with social work managers' (Lymbery, 1998: 863). This raises questions in respect of the extent to which a similar emphasis in children's services on formalised 'assessment frameworks', procedural requirements and time constraints contribute to the de-professionalisation of the social worker's role in children's social work. Rogowski (2008) makes a similar point, noting that 'managerialism now bedevils social work entailing as it does a focus on bureaucracy such as form filling and assessments, leaving little time for face to face work with children and families' (Rogowski, 2008: 17). Combined with the requirement for managers to counter sign and authorise assessments, reports and care plans, the procedural requirements of assessment frameworks and Integrated Children's Systems have served to decrease the autonomy and professionalism of the individual social worker and reduce their ability and willingness to exercise their professional and legal powers effectively in some cases. For Rogowski:

> . . . *social workers themselves, at the instigation of managers, now have to focus on targets, performance indicators and filling in forms and questionnaires. Professionally led practice based on knowledge, skills and experience, occupational identity and collegial relations, autonomy and discretion have been replaced by so-called professionalism based on organisational rather than professional values emphasising bureaucratic/ managerial controls, including budgetary restrictions and financial rationalisations and requires the standardisation of practices.*

Rogowski, 2008: 22

Similarly, research by Broadhurst et al. (2010) found that the very systems designed to safeguard children had the effect, in practice, of reducing social workers contact with children. These systems also led to hasty 'categorisations' of cases in order to provide 'timely' responses with workers reporting their concern at the ease with which they could lose sight of their primary role to support and safeguard in their need to meet performance targets.

In his discussion of the tension between the discourses of welfare, law and managerialism, Dickens (2008) also examines their similarities and differences and the effects that these discourses have had in social work practice with children and families. He argues that the three elements of welfare, law and managerialism are bound together in practice but that the three discourses also remain separate, in a dynamic relationship coming together to promote the interests of the child but also each retaining their own rationale and sometimes conflicting drivers. He observed that:

> . . . *in local authority social work the tensions are not just between law and welfare. Issues of resource management, procedural compliance and organisational structure are also prominent, and may well be dominant in the minds of field-level practitioners.*

Dickens, 2008: 49

Dickens' research involved interviews with social workers, lawyers and managers and sought to understand the perspectives of each group of the other. For front line social workers there was a tension between appreciating the help provided by lawyers, sometimes based on a lack of guidance from managers, and concerns about legal involvement in a case. Other tensions centred on either over or under involvement of lawyers in particular cases. In discussing these issues with practising social workers one gave an example of a Local Authority lawyer attempting to instruct a social worker in Court, the social worker stated 'the lawyer was focused solely on the letter of the law without taking into account the full picture of my assessment and risk awareness'.

Lawyers similarly expressed concern about why they were consulted in some cases, believing that the questions asked of them centred on 'welfare' and were management and supervisory questions rather than legal concerns. In such cases lawyers cited the lack of experience, or of more concern, lack of knowledge on the part of the social worker. Some lawyers however saw little distinction between matters of law and matters of welfare in child care cases. Lawyers in the study were often critical of management concerns with budgets and this was reciprocated by the managers in the study reporting 'resentment' of lawyers' apparent 'over-involvement' in cases, both on the ground of budgetary concerns and a perceived undermining of their role and expertise, as Dickens (2008: 57) notes; 'guarding the boundaries of their role as well as their budget'.

In this context it is not difficult to see how the front line social worker might feel either propelled into or prevented from using their legal powers, depending on their own knowledge of the law and the support available to them at the time. From a managerial perspective a 'concern to avoid unnecessary expenditure can help to keep a case out of court proceedings; but equally too dominant a concern with saving money risks leaving children without the services or protection they need' (Dickens, 2008: 59).

Social work power and the law

This perspective therefore clearly underlines the practitioner's need to be confident in their knowledge and application of the law. Statutory social work is shaped by and framed within a set of legal powers and duties the basis for which is to be found in the *Local Authority Social Services Act 1970*, which requires local authorities to provide for social services functions. Several of the provisions of this founding legislation have been changed, particularly in respect of children's services, in response to developments in delivery of services and as a result of legislative and structural changes such as the merging of the children's social care and education functions of local authorities (Brammer, 2010). Some might argue that this again underlines the rise of managerial concerns rather than professional drivers informing policy and practice. Legislative and policy changes arising out of recent child death enquiries might also be seen to be 'managerial' rather than practice driven. Changes arising from the Laming enquiry (Victoria Climbié, *Every Child Matters*, 2004) in the form of the *Children Act 2004*, established the post of Children's Commissioner for England, emphasised improved inter-agency communication, the setting up of Local Safeguarding Children Boards (LSCB), and the introduction of a common assessment framework (CAF) to be used by the whole of the children's workforce, not just social workers. The *Children Act 2004* therefore focuses on strengthening preventative services and introduced organisational and structural changes designed to bring about improvements in inter-agency working with the aim of reinforcing the legal framework for safeguarding children and protecting them from harm. The *Children and Young Persons Act 2008* provides the legislative framework for improving services for children and young people in the 'care system', focusing more explicitly on practice and provision of services, strengthening the role of the Independent Reviewing Officer (IRO) and placing new duties on local authorities, for example to ensure that children and young people looked after by the local authority receive visits and that services are tailored to their needs. Social work legislation therefore provides the mandate for practitioners to assess and intervene but the relationship between law and social work remains a contested one (Braye and Preston-Shoot, 2010). On the one hand practitioners are criticised for over zealous application of their legal powers (Cleveland, 1988) and on the other for failing to act with sufficient speed or rigour (Victoria Climbié, 2003; Baby Peter, 2009). In the Baby Peter case in particular, it was found that there was a very clear audit trail but all it demonstrated was how the Local Authority and other professionals had failed to protect the vulnerable child. As Preston-Shoot notes (2001: 11) '. . . reliance on procedures allows practitioners to distance themselves from dilemmas and emotions encountered in practice, and to decline responsibility for the outcomes that are sought and the process by which they are to be realised'. The social worker's power is also mediated by managers who countersign, and sometimes change, a social worker's report before it goes to court. The issue of ownership of the assessment and conclusion of the report are therefore diluted if the social worker no longer sees their own intervention and assessment reflected in the final report as presented to the court.

Added to this potent mix is the way in which agency policies and requirements are often seen as more important in practice than the legal rules from which they might derive. Again as Preston-Shoot (2001: 53) observed 'Practitioners are inducted into agency policy procedure and practice, as if it is the picture'. It is perhaps then unsurprising that social workers often perceive themselves to have an ambivalent relationship to the legal rules. Research focusing on the teaching and assessment of law in practice learning by Braye et al. (2007) confirmed that this ambivalence is still prevalent in practice. As it was asserted that:

The lack of explicitness, or of overt use of the law to inform practice, tends to create a dependency on agency policies and procedures rather than the legal rules themselves. This often has the effect of discouraging . . . practitioners from examining the legal rules and encourages a reliance on agency policies as guiding principles for practice.

Braye et al., 2007: 330

Also noting, in respect of how students are supported to learn about the law, that:

There was a danger, when identifying legal rules relevant to the agency context, of focusing only on those mandating a narrow range of interventions carried out by the team in question, missing opportunities to make links between law and rights in the broader context of service users' lives. Equally, there were experiences of legal rules being prioritised within the agency context when they supported something an agency wished to do, such as rationing services, and not referred to where they might support service users' rights.

Braye et al., 2007: 329

It appears from this research that practitioners responsible for students on placement are guiding students to consider agency policy and procedure as the 'correct' approach with law only being referred to if it assists the agency in achieving its own goals. If this is students' experience during their social work training then it is perhaps no surprise that the practitioners they become have difficulty in being law centred and making use of the full extent of their powers in the face of organisational culture and managerial goals. The focus in practice therefore on 'doing' rather than thinking undermines the connections between a social worker's lawful use of power and the underpinning legal rules.

Decision making and use of power

Decision making in social work practice is governed by administrative law and, within this, the provisions of the European Convention on Human Rights as integrated into UK law through the *Human Rights Act 1998*. Within this context 'blanket decisions', for example to prohibit more expensive 'out of county' placements for young people in care, are rendered unlawful (R v Gloucestershire CC, ex parte Barry [1997] 2All ER1). The social worker, whose assessment clearly identifies grounds for such a placement to meet the needs of the young person whose needs cannot be met within local resources, therefore has the backing of the principles of administrative law in respect of decision making to argue for such provision.

Practitioners also have to manage the tension between lawful decision making, i.e. in accordance with the statutory mandate and action which may be inhumane or unethical in terms of the impact on service users. In the case of F (A Child) [2008] EWCA Civ 439 the

Local Authority was found to have acted unethically, although within the letter of the law, in ignoring the last minute request of a biological father to contest the adoption of his child. Braye and Preston-Shoot (2006) identify three orientations to law knowledge which should inform a practitioner's application of their legal powers. These are identified as rational/technical, moral/ethical and rights/justice. They argue that a balance between the three strands is necessary to ensure lawful and ethical practice, locating the rights of the service user central to the decision making. In practice, however, the pressure from managers is often to obey the 'letter of the law' as the case example cited above suggests, without locating this in the context of rights, justice and value based practice.

The *Human Rights Act 1998* requires that public authorities act in accordance with the principles of the European Convention on Human Rights. For a social worker on the front line therefore it is essential that they understand and use their legal powers in such a way as to both respect and promote service users' rights to a fair trial (article 6), family life (article 8), protection from inhuman treatment (article 3) (Preston-Shoot, 2000; Welbourne, 2010). In order to do this, they must be clear about issues of proportionality, the limits of rights which are defined as 'qualified' and be skilled in arguing how and why such rights must be upheld or breached in specific cases. This clearly requires them to move beyond a narrow understanding and application of agency policies and procedure to develop a critically enquiring and reflective stance on both practice and the legal rules that mandate them to act.

The decisions which social workers are required to make therefore involves a complex interplay of theoretical and legal knowledge and practice wisdom within an ethical framework of explicit social work values, applied with a high level of skill and self-awareness. Lymbery (1998: 865) argues that 'social work has not been successful in articulating the complex and sophisticated professional judgements which underpin its practice'. The increased emphasis on 'technical solutions' therefore through formalised procedures and recording systems increases the risk of social workers taking an approach based on 'technical rationality' rather than a reflective approach to complex and 'messy' practice situations (Schon, 1983). Such technical approaches tend to distance the social worker from the reflexive 'use of self' which underpins professional social work practice and decision making. The preoccupation in practice and supervision with targets and deadlines therefore can distract the social work practitioner from their core task which is to:

> . . . *assess the problems confronting the service user then make a judgement about the coping capacity of the service user and the resources (internal and external) available to that person, and finally make an informed judgement about the most appropriate way to assist the service user to resolve the problems.*
>
> Lymbery, 1998: 867

The issues of ownership of decision making and accountability are therefore key to ensuring that the social worker is able to take into account all of the factors affecting the situation, but may be reduced if the front-line social worker is distanced from the decision by a perceived lack of ownership of the basis of the decision, i.e. the social worker is the object of a hierarchical, procedural and regulatory approach to decision making rather than a subject actively engaged in the process. As Preston-Shoot notes:

> ... *whilst regulation may impact in general practice standards and introduce greater consistency, rule dominated behaviour will not resolve the moral questions and practice dilemmas faced by the social worker ... reliance on procedures and preoccupation with performance indicators may place 'clients' at risk.*
>
> Preston-Shoot, 2001: 10–1

Similarly Banks (2004: 149) refers to what she terms the 'new accountability' which she defines as the 'development of increasingly detailed procedures for doing tasks and the setting of predefined targets or outcomes for work'. This she identifies as reducing the practitioners' ability to exercise professional autonomy through the use of discretion and decision making. Blacher (2003) writing about the role of the out of hours social worker notes that this area of work does not have the same managerial hierarchy of consultation and decision making as is experienced in day time services. He argues therefore that this provides out of hours workers with 'an enhanced sense of personal responsibility and a different kind of accountability which can seem more personal and more individual ... a different kind of professionalism' (Blacher, 2003: 67). It can be argued therefore that greater regulation and tighter control on the actions and decisions of the individual social worker has the effect of distancing them from the effects of their actions/ inaction and therefore decreases their sense of both professionalism and accountability.

In a further comparison with Emergency Duty Team (EDT) workers, Blacher (2003) notes that out of hours workers are much more likely than daytime workers to work routinely alongside the police. He further reports that for EDT workers, 'in situations needing the involvement of more than one work ... the assistance of the police rather than another social worker is likely to be requested' (Blacher, 2003: 64). One of the criticisms of Haringey's practices in the Laming report was that it appeared that the social workers there had a hostile difficult and untrusting relationship with the police, (Laming, 2003). One might question therefore whether a shared sense of responsibility with the police, and the more overt alignment with an explicitly 'controlling' service, renders the social worker's use of their own powers more immediately accessible. The involvement of the police routinely in social work situations should however be viewed with caution. The potential for oppression and heavy-handedness in such an approach needs to be balanced against the requirement for social workers to own their responsibilities for action and the use of their available powers.

Reflective practice and the use of power

For professionals working in such a context of uncertainty and competing organisational goals, the role of reflective practice is crucial in order to maintain professional integrity. Reflective practice, focusing as it does on the complex interplay of personal and professional identity, knowledge and theory, values, ethics and the worker's use of self, allows the practitioner to own their actions, and to locate issues of need, risk, strength, power and procedure within a framework of defensible, and not defensive practice. Much of what has been discussed above therefore points to the need for greater levels of clinical and reflective supervision to assist decision making and ensure that powers are appropriately and effectively used, rather than a bureaucratic emphasis on targets and procedures that currently epitomise the practitioner/ manager relationship in many cases. In the final report of the Social Work Task Force (2009b: 31) it is noted that; *'high quality reflective supervision is essential to achieving a fair and balanced workload'* and also that:

> In order to make a real difference to those they work with, social workers need high quality professional supervision and time for reflective practice and continuing professional development.
>
> Social Work Task Force, 2009b: 65

Reflective practice may be described as an active process of constructing solutions using knowledge, experience and learning rather than a passive process of following set procedures. Schon describes reflective practice as practice in which the practitioner engages in a 'reflective conversation with the situation' (Schon, 1983: 163) Such an approach requires practitioners to engage with the complexity of a case, identifying and addressing both their own impact on the situation (use of self) and the impact of the work on themselves. Mandell (2008) explores the use of self in relation to child welfare work, focusing specifically on the power dimensions of the worker-service user relationship. She argues that the worker's social location and identity impacts on their understanding and use of power in the professional relationship but that the power dimension is absent from many theoretical explorations of use of self.

The reflective practitioner therefore needs to take into account their own impact on the situation as well as the needs, strengths, risks and statutory requirements in the given situation. Clinical rather than managerial supervision can provide a reflective space for both the practitioner and manager to engage with issues of complexity and enable the appropriate use of power and authority by locating it both within the procedural and professional practice arena, thus producing tailored responses. By contrast, assessment and review documentation that are increasingly prescribed and uniform are likely to generate standardised responses. The Integrated Children's System (ICS) has been criticised for being repetitive, excessively bureaucratic and has the effect of preventing practitioners from providing a holistic narrative account, (Social Work Task Force, 2009a, 2009b; Broadhurst et al., 2010). As one social worker explained to the author, 'it is very difficult to find the history (of a case) in ICS'. For reflective practitioners the process of narration, either verbally or in writing, can reveal new understandings and insights into a situation in a way that inputting standardised responses into a proforma document cannot do. The process of writing taps 'tacit knowledge' (Schon, 1987) and allows the practitioner to develop a deeper understanding of the situation. Prescribed responses and proforma recording methods therefore militate against reflective practice. The findings of the Social Work Task Force (2009b: 34) suggest that the Integrated Children's System, 'should be reformed so that it supports effective record-keeping and case management by social workers' and also recommends the development of peer and group supervision including the space for focused and reflective case discussion.

The need therefore is to ensure that alongside 'managerial' supervision, space is created for reflective or clinical supervision focusing on practice issues, dilemmas and concerns. This is acknowledged by Peter Lewis, head of Children's Services in the London Borough of Haringey, who in an interview with Community Care (March 2010) highlighting the improvements in that authority since the death of Baby Peter, stated that social work practitioners feel better able to perform with confidence when they are supported by managers who take an interest both in the work they do and themselves as workers.

Fook and Gardner (2007: 150) note that managers, as well as front-line practitioners, also benefit from critical reflection stating that *'critical reflection does offer managers a process for considering organisational issues in a way that respects the knowledge and experience of those at all levels of the organisation'*. They further argue that critical reflection can also be helpful to managers who face conflicting pressures in their day to day work, firstly the managerial pressures of processes and routines to minimise risk and maximise budgets and secondly the pressure to create and be part of a 'learning organisation'. This can clearly be seen in children's services in the twin drivers of increased regulation and frameworks for assessment and recording, alongside an emphasis on the continuous professional development of the workforce through, newly qualified social worker programmes, post-qualifying training (GSCC) and the proposed new Masters level qualification in Social Work Practice. In recognition of this complexity, the Social Work Task Force has also recommended the development of tailored training programmes for the managers of front line social workers, (Social Work Task Force, 2009b).

Conclusion

It is clear that the tragedy of two child deaths in a single local authority has highlighted failings in a system designed to protect children and support families. In both cases, social workers on the front-line have been criticised, as have the dysfunctional systems within which they were found to be working. In both cases the roles of other professionals have also been criticised but the most virulent criticism has been reserved for the social workers and their managers, for failing to effectively use their statutory and professional powers. It may be argued that the social work profession had both the power and mandate to intervene and either did not, or not with sufficient rigour. The echoes with previous tragedies (Maria Colwell, 1974; Jasmine Beckford, 1985; Kimberley Carlisle, 1987; Tyra Henry, 1987) are clear. The rise of managerialism over this time appears to have made little improvement to the outcomes of social workers' practice, and impacted negatively by contributing to the 'reduction of professional confidence and pride, producing feelings of being de-skilled and de-valued' (Thompson, 2010: 51).

The Social Work Task Force Report (2009b) makes a range of recommendations for reform and improvement, not just of the social work profession itself, but also the way in which it is perceived by the public. Amongst its many observations, the need for high quality professional/ clinical supervision and time for reflective practice and continuing professional development are clear, and to be welcomed. If social workers are to be empowered to make effective use of their statutory and professional powers, then giving them the space, and the tools, for both lawful and reflective practice is crucial, as is ensuring that they develop the skills and knowledge to apply these effectively.

The Laming Report (2003) Care Matters: Time for Change (DfES, 2007) and the Social Work Task Force Report (2009b) have all focused on the need to strengthen initial social work training and early professional development. The overall thrust of many of the recommendations arising from these reports would appear to call into question, either implicitly or explicitly, the relevance of qualifying training for the role and task of the social worker in practice. It is true that the attention in qualifying social work education is, in line with the Department of Health Requirements for Social Work Training (2002) focused on inter-personal and 'human' skills as well as knowledge of assessment, law, human development and inter-professional working. We have also seen that there is a disjuncture between, for example, the teaching of law in the academic arena and how it is distorted by a focus on agency policy and procedures in practice. All of these reports (Laming, 2003; DfES, 2007; SWTF, 2009b) also point to the need for social workers to spend more time with children and families, for which the necessary skills lie in communication, assessment and a sound understanding of child development, family and power dynamics, and the relevant legal rules. For many front-line social workers however, as we have seen, their reality is marked by limited direct contact with children, young people and their families and an organisational emphasis on IT systems and 'paperwork' with much of their time spent in the office, inputting data into a computer. Is it therefore the case that their education and training at qualifying and post-qualifying level is not 'fit for purpose' or is it that the expectations of front line social workers in practice have been distorted by the burden of bureaucracy and the rise of managerialism impacting negatively on their ability to use their knowledge, skills and power to best effect?

References

Banks, S. (2004) *Ethics, Accountability and the Social Professions*. Basingstoke, Palgrave Macmillan.

Blacher, M. (2003) The Autonomous Practitioner? Out of Hours/EDT Practice and 'Mainstream'/ Daytime Practice: Some Points of Divergence. *Practice*, 15: 2, 59–70.

Brammer, A. (2010) *Social Work Law*. Harlow, Longman.

Braye, S. and Preston-Shoot, M. (2006) *Teaching, Learning and Assessment of Law in Social Work Education*. Bristol, Social Care Institute for Excellence.

Braye, S. Preston-Shoot, M. and Thorpe, A. (2007) Beyond the Classroom: Learning Social Work Law in Practice. *Journal of Social Work*, 7: 3, 322–40.

Braye, S. and Preston-Shoot, M. (2010) *Practising Social Work Law*. 3rd. edn. London, Macmillan.

Brechin, A., Brown, H. et al. (2000) *Critical Practice in Health and Social Care*. London, Sage.

Broadhurst, K. et al. (2010) Performing 'Initial Assessment': Identifying the Latent Conditions for Error at the Front-Door of Local Authority Children's Services. *British Journal of Social Work*, 40, 352–70.

Cooper, J. (2010) Back on Track after Baby P. *Community Care*, 04 March.

DfES (2004) *Every Child Matters: Change for Children*. London, HMSO.

DfES (2007) *Care Matters: Time for Change*. Nottingham, DfES.

DoH (2002) *Requirements for Social Work Training*. London, HMSO.

Dickens, J. (2008) Welfare, Law and Managerialsim: Inter-discursivity and Interprofessional Practice in child Care Social Work. *Journal of Social Work*, 8: 1, 45–64.

Eby, M. (2000) In Brechin, A., Brown, H. et al. (2000) *Critical Practice in Health and Social Care*. London, Sage.

Fook, J. and Gardner, F. (2007) *Practising Critical Reflection. A Resource Handbook*. Maidenhead, Open University Press, McGraw Hill Educational.

Hugman, R. (1991) *Power in the Caring Professions*. Basingstoke, Macmillan.

Laming, Lord H. (2003) *The Victoria Climbié Enquiry: Report of an Inquiry by Lord Laming*. London, HMSO.

Laming, H. (2009) *The Protection of Children in England: A Progress Report*. London, HMSO.

Long, L., Roche, J. and Stringer, D. (2010) *The Law and Social Work: Contemporary Issues for Practice*. Basingstoke, Palgrave Macmillan.

Lukes, S. (2005) *Power, A Radical View*. 2nd edn. Basingstoke, Palgrave Macmillan.

Lymbery, M. (1998) Care Management and Professional Autonomy: The Impact of Community Care on Social Work with Older People. *British Journal of Social Work*, 28, 863–78.

Jones, C. (2001) Voices from the Front Line: State Social Work and New Labour. *British Journal of Social Work*, 31, 547–62.

Mandell, D. (2008) Power, Care and Vulnerability: Considering Use of Self In Child Welfare Work. *Journal of Social Work Practice*, 22: 2, 235–48.

Preston-Shoot, M. (2000) What if? Using the Law to Uphold Practice Values and Standards. *Practice*, 12: 4, 49–63.

Preston-Shoot, M. (2001) Regulating the Road of Good Intentions: Observations on The Relationship Between Policy, Regulations and Practice In Social Work. *Practice*, 13: 4, 5–20.

Rogowski, S. (2008) Social Work with Children and Families: Towards a Radical Practice. *Practice: Social Work in Action*, 20: 1, 17–28.

Schön, D.A. (1983) *The Reflective Practitioner*. New York, Basic Books.

Schön, D.A. (1987) *Educating the Reflective Practitioner*. Jossey-Bass, San Francisco.

Smith, R. (2008) *Social Work and Power*. Basingstoke, Palgrave Macmillan.

Tew, J. (2002) *Social Theory, Power and Practice*. Basingstoke, Palgrave Macmillan.

Tew, J. (2006) Understanding Power and Powerlessness: Towards a Framework for Emancipatory Practice in Social Work. *Journal of Social Work*, 6: 1, 33–51.

The Social Work Task Force (2009a) *Facing up to the Task: The Interim Report of the Social Work Task Force*. London, HMSO.

The Social Work Task Force (2009b) *Building a Safe Confident Future: The Final Report of the Social Work Task Force*. London, HMSO.

Thompson, N. (2001) *Anti-Discriminatory Practice*. London, Palgrave Macmillan.

Thompson, N. (2003) *Promoting Equality*. Basingstoke, Macmillan.

Thompson, N. (2010) *Theorising Social Work Practice*. London, Palgrave Macmillan.

Welbourne, P. (2010) Accountability. In Long, L., Roche, J. and Stringer, D. (2010) *The Law and Social Work: Contemporary Issues for Practice*. Basingstoke, Palgrave Macmillan.

Westwood, S. (2002) *Power and the Social*. London, Routledge.

CHAPTER 8

Social Work in Schools

Andrew Brown

Introduction

Schools go to great lengths to find ways of supporting those children who have difficulty coping and social work is just one form of support that is increasingly being incorporated into the school setting. This chapter will examine the role of social work in a school setting and explore the impact that that role can have on children, families and the school community. It will also look at the implications for the practitioner in such settings. For the purpose of clarity, when referring to the school social worker in this chapter it is a reference to a social worker employed by a school as oppose to a social worker attached to a school from the local authority or statutory social services team. This distinction is necessary as the statutory duties differ quite considerably between the two. Furthermore, my personal experience will form the basis for the ideas put forward in this chapter and I will draw particular attention to the elements I think have been important in my role as a school social worker.

People interpret and respond to their environment in different ways and when children are responding to their school environment, their experiences can be vastly different. School can be the most joyous, stimulating and creative place for some children. For these children it is a place where they are able to be free to explore and learn about who they are, where they have come from, who else exists apart from themselves and what other possibilities may lie ahead. It is a place of learning and intellectual development and it is also a place where their emotional, psychological and physical maturation are allowed to flourish. However; despite all these positive attributes the school environment can also be the most fearful, stressful and dreaded place for others. At its worst it can be the most frightening environment, where ones sense of instability, uncertainty and emotional and psychological fragility is laid bare. A place where there is no protection from hostility, brutality and the vindictiveness of others. How a child experiences school can be attributed to a broad range of factors, including the school environment itself and its structures (including protective ones) systems and processes, the child's home circumstances, their relationship with their peer group as well as the state of their physical, psychological and emotional health and well being. These different factors, to a varying degree, all impact on the way children experience their school life.

There is little doubt about the importance of the early childhood years, as children spend the most formative part of their lives in school. The contribution that these formative years make towards determining the outcomes and opportunities for children in later life is beyond doubt. So what does this mean for those children whose circumstances create barriers that prevent them from fully engaging with their education and school environment in general? Surely for these children the school experience is even more crucial since, as some would argue that, their outcomes and opportunities are already limited. If a school can intervene at an early stage to nurture those young minds, who are already facing difficulties and potentially developing a negative perception of themselves and the world around them, would it be possible to reduce the negative effects those difficult circumstances can have on the developing child? Looking at research findings, Blyth and Milner (1997) have said, 'various research studies, conducted in a number of different countries, have shown that positive school experiences can not only provide support to children in adverse social circumstances but even help to counter their impact' (Blyth and Milner, 1997: 14). Although somewhat dated, I would argue nevertheless, that the Blyth and Milner 1997 finding is still of relevance.

With so much at stake for individuals and with so much potential to shape future society through its young people, recent education reforms have rightly attempted to improve the standard of education generally and for children looked after by the state in particular. There has been a greater emphasis placed on curriculum development, achievement, measurability and accountability. Raising the standard of education and helping a child to achieve means supporting the increase in the quality of teaching and learning. This in turn, it is hoped, would automatically raise the expectations of children in school. The view is that if what is being delivered is of better quality and is more accessible, then children should be able to achieve higher academic levels and better results. It is accepted that raising the expectations of children in school is necessary in order to help them to achieve the best of their ability. However, many children find it difficult to cope with the demands of school and this is more apparent when the child has difficult familial circumstances and other individual problems that impinge on their life and their ability to engage with school. These children are often measured as achieving at levels below the national average. But in order for a child to reach their full potential and for them to come away with an overall positive school experience, they will need a great deal of guidance and support. The challenge for all schools, I would argue, is both to create the necessary learning environment but also to try and provide the appropriate support as effectively as possible.

Meeting the needs of children: the legal dimension

The direction of the education system, although a very separate entity in some ways, recognises the need to provide additional services to children and their families and is supported by initiatives in children centres and by the Common Assessment Framework. Such initiatives are working towards early intervention and prevention and are guided by the *Every Child Matters Agenda* (2003) (ECM). The ultimate aim is to work collectively to address children's social and emotional needs and enable them to achieve their full potential. The ECM agenda also directly contributes to education setting by outlining five outcomes for children, which every school and other agencies are expected (must) to promote. The outcomes includes: *be healthy, stay safe, enjoy and achieve, make a positive contribution and achieve economic well-being*.

To a large extent the death of Victoria Climbié was the catalyst for the creation of ECM and the need for those in contact with children to intervene early in order to prevent future tragedies. The *Every Child Matters* green paper, which was published alongside Lord Laming's report into the death of Victoria Climbié observed that:

> *Victoria Climbié came into contact with several agencies, none of which acted on the warning signs. No one built up the full picture of her interactions with different services. Children with problems such as special educational needs, or behavioural disorders, or suffering from neglect, can also find that services often come too late. This Green Paper sets out the long term vision for how we intend to intervene earlier.*
>
> *Every Child Matters*, 2003: 51

This statement marked a shift in government and local authorities as it ushered a move towards implementing more early intervention and preventative services. The responsibilities of local authorities to protect children from harm are clearly defined in policy, guidance and legislation but where does the school social workers duty lie in relation to legislation and statutory obligations?

The *Children Act 1989* and *2004*, *Education Act 2002*, *Every Child Matters* and *Working Together to Safeguard Children* are important documents because they place requirements on agencies to intervene and safeguard children. The *Children Act 1989* and *2004* underpins the duties and responsibilities of social workers and charges them with powers to assess, support and protect children from significant harm. Compulsory assessments have to be carried out by a local authority social worker and not the school social worker although they are carried out jointly on many occasions. Section 27 (1–3) and 47 (9–11) of the *Children Act 1989* also places a duty on schools (and all other relevant agencies) to cooperate with assessments or enquiries being made. *Children Act 2004* extended this duty by requiring co-operation in order to 'improve the well-being of children as measured by five outcomes', which brings it in line with the Every Child Matters agenda. Furthermore:

Section 11 of the Children Act 2004, section 175 of the Education Act 2002 and section 55 of the Borders, Citizenship and Immigration Act 2009 place duties on organisations and individuals to ensure that their functions are discharged with regard to the need to safeguard and promote the welfare of children.

Working Together to Safeguard Children, 2006: 9

So how does this legislation and guidance translate in practice for the school social worker? The school social worker's statutory duties lie within the realms of the expectations on all schools when children are at risk of significant harm. If there are concerns of abuse or neglect raised about a child then these must be referred to social services for assessment. However, this does not always mean that an assessment will be carried out and the decision may be that the concerns are not great enough to meet the threshold for assessment or intervention. This decision is a source of conflict as professional opinions often differ between social services and other agencies but ultimately, in these instances, the school (or referring agency) is responsible for intervening. As Working Together to Safeguard Children states:

Schools (including independent and non-maintained schools) and further education institutions have a duty to safeguard and promote the welfare of pupils under the Education Act 2002. They should create and maintain a safe learning environment for children and young people, and identify where there are child welfare concerns and take action to address them, in partnership with other organisations where appropriate.

Working together to Safeguard Children, 2006: 11

Statutory services intervene when there are serious or potentially serious risks to children and so the service is focused on addressing more specialist needs. To best explain the school social workers position the diagram below (see Figure 8.1), relates to the continuum of need.

On the left of the diagram are universal needs that all children have and are generally met by parents, school and the wider community. As you move to the right of the diagram the needs of the child or family become greater. Additional needs and some complex needs would be met through early intervention, common assessment framework and the team around the child, More complex and some specialist needs would be met through Section 17 of the *Children Act 1989* and 2004 when a child would be assessed as a Child in Need and a subsequent plan would be put in place to address those needs. More specialist needs are where serious risks to children are present and are addressed by children being subject to a child protection plan. Typically, the school social worker would be more involved (and

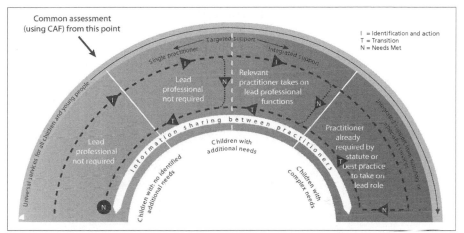

www.staffordshirechildrenstrust.org.uk

Figure 8.1   The continuum of need

sometimes solely responsible for) additional and complex needs. However; I believe the school social worker has an essential role to play right across the continuum of need.

Children are seen on a daily basis within school so early warning signs and additional needs can be recognised and picked up quickly. If a family has more complex or specialists needs the situation can be closely monitored and support and advice given almost immediately. When potential risks to children are recognised these can be acted upon quickly. Working in partnership with outside agencies is an essential part of this work and determines how quickly and effectively a problem can be responded to. When statutory social services become involved with a family one of the most common complaints is that the allocated worker does not stay long and there is a great turnover of social workers. For the family, this often means starting again each time the Social Worker changes, which can lead to feelings of resentment and that nothing is being done. This can make it even more difficult for the next practitioner to engage with the family, form positive relationships and for the family to readily accept help. The reasons for frequent changes in some cases are many but as a school social worker it is possible to remain involved with a family and be a consistent person, before, during and beyond a crisis.

Social work in a school environment

The cohort of a school and the socio-cultural and socio-economic environment within which it operates are important to consider when examining the role of social work in a school setting. What the work would entail and the nature of the problems that are likely to be presented would be very much shaped by these factors. The work of a social worker in school is varied and multifaceted. In my experience, the scope of the types of services a social worker can offer in a school is extremely broad and for this reason the role is ever changing. How the role is developed within the school relies a great deal on what the management team expects of a social worker. However, because of the difference in professional training and thinking, the practitioner has an opportunity to promote and utilise the difference in approach and bring new skills and ideas when planning for and providing support to children and their families. Ultimately, the focus of social work in a school is on early intervention and prevention however in practice the role broadens out to include multiple types of work. Some examples of the types of services a school social worker can offer are:

- Counselling can be provided for children and their families and can cover a wide range of issues including academic performance, disabilities, domestic violence, emotional and behavioural difficulties and other personal issues.
- Advising children and their parents in relation to difficulties they may be facing, options available to them and signposting to other services. Advice can also be given to teachers and other school staff particularly when children are adversely affected by their circumstances.
- Practical support can be provided in many ways and forms a large part of the work in a school. Some examples include, facilitating children to actively resolve conflicts for themselves; helping parents to access additional services (including benefits) and fill in forms; coordinating family support, mental health and other services within the home and school; small group work covering topics of social skills and anger management and advising on behaviour management and communication strategies.
- Mediation between children, parents and the school is a regular feature of social work in schools when there are disagreements.
- Crisis intervention is another key role within a school. Family disputes, domestic violence, homelessness, bullying and financial troubles are just some of the issues that require an immediate response and are usually dealt with by the school social worker.
- Child protection is an area that requires great stringency in its policies and practices and a school social worker is well placed to pick up on and confidently deal with concerns that are raised.
- Advocating on behalf of children and families in different situations.
- Mentoring can also be carried out by a school social worker which usually involves working in groups and on a one-to-one basis with children and supporting them to fully engage with their education.

The work is very varied and rewarding and it requires a positive outlook and the ability to take initiatives. Most important it requires a belief in the human potential and people's ability to change. The practitioner must be flexible in their work and be able to respond appropriately in situations where they may well be the only qualified social welfare professional involved. This type of work is based on a supportive model aiming to empower people to find solutions to problems through building and maintaining positive relationships. However, the practitioner must be cautious not to over-identify with a family or situation and as a result give people the benefit of doubt when there are potential risks to children. In a school setting, a lot of work is done to develop positive relationships and promote partnership working but difficult decisions often need to be made that could potentially damage those relationships. The practitioner, in my view, needs to remain objective and hone their skills to ensure the correct judgments are made at the right time. This is something many people working in the field of children and families are aware of but because the role of school social worker is still relatively uncommon there may not be a support structure in place in comparison to what one may find in a statutory setting. Supervision may not be delivered in the same way and is likely to be provided by a person from an education perspective rather than social work. In a school setting a school social worker does not have immediate access to other social workers in the field to share practice ideas. Also despite being in the same borough but because of the setting one may not be able to refer directly to services commissioned by the borough. This means the school social worker is somewhat isolated in their work and unless they are proactive and innovative they are unlikely to access a range of services and support for the children and their families. I have found, through networking and researching, it is possible to creatively source and implement different types of services and support. It is also essential to be highly reflective and to seek out opportunities to participate in relevant training and share good practice with others in order to enhance assessment and decision making skills.

School culture and ethos

The ethos of a school is important in determining the environment in which children can learn and develop to their full potential. As Blyth and Milner (1997) observed 'The effects of schools on their pupils as both children and adults have been extensively studied, the consistent finding from both the research being that pupils' academic progress varies greatly according to the school they attend' (Blyth and Milner, 1997: 13). The expectation of the standard of education a school should provide is consistent, however the way in which a school achieves this standard ultimately lies with the school's leadership team. The leadership team shapes the ethos of a school through its policies, procedures and practices and the decisions made on what is important in order to create a positive and effective learning environment can differ from school to school. The vision and ideology of the leadership team is the main driving force behind the development of a school ethos and environment, however it can also be influenced by the demography of an area and the intake of children into a school through its catchment. For example, in an area with high rates of migrates, disability, crime, teenage pregnancy, low income and social housing, the local school may find they have higher than average numbers of pupils who have a range of special educational needs; who do not speak English as a first language; who have behavioural and emotional difficulties; have unsettled or even traumatic home lives and live in overcrowded or unsuitable accommodation. Because of these challenges the school environment will need to adapt in order to effectively provide the appropriate support to address the high levels of need amongst its pupils. The school may decide that an extensive pastoral team is required and use their budget to create a staff structure that enables them to address the needs effectively. This could consist of language support, learning mentors, school counsellors, behaviour support assistants, social workers, therapists, charity organisations and any other agency providing a supportive service to children. By placing an emphasis on high levels of support and inclusivity (as well as academic abilities) it could mean a move towards a more open and therapeutic school environment as opposed to one of an authoritarian or disciplinarian nature. The point here is not to say that one approach is more effective than the other, as it is more common that schools perform better if different types of approach co-exist, but simply that the decisions made by schools can be somewhat dictated by its cohort.

Multi-agency working and the power dynamics

Some hold the view that social work in schools is not 'proper' social work. However, my experience would suggest that such views ignores, undermines and devalues the work that is done to prevent many children and families reaching crisis point. Is 'proper' social work responding to high-risk situations and crisis on behalf of the state to ensure the safety and well-being of vulnerable people? Is it engaging with and befriending individuals, families and communities in order to work towards positive change? Is it helping people? Is it collectively utilising the knowledge and skills of multiple professionals to thoroughly assess, support and make decisions with, and on behalf of individuals and families? In my view these elements, and so many more, are present in the practice of social work regardless of the setting. Early intervention services not only prevent the risk of harm to individuals but also prevent a further strain on the people dealing with high-risk situations by avoiding crisis. Likewise, when a Local Authority takes ultimate responsibility for a high-risk situation this allows early intervention services to continue the preventative work and still play an important role.

There are however clear distinctions to be made between school social workers and Local Authority social workers. The most important distinction, which this book aims to explore, is the responsibility for the use of powers. There is no doubting that school social workers do not have the same legal powers as their local authority counterparts. Responsibility for insisting that a statutory assessment or child protection investigation is carried out; and applications for residence or care orders, lies with local authority social care teams. Being charged with the responsibility to use powers is one thing but the approach one takes towards the use of those powers is where the skill and the art of the profession comes to the fore. Decisions to use powers are made on an individual basis, however different people can look at the same situation and see different risks. This leaves room for interpretation and is also where tensions can lie in agreeing how and when powers should be exercised. Looking at social work training and much of the guidance literature for the profession, there is a huge emphasis placed on building positive relationships and providing support in order to keep families together (this particular point is considered by Sarah Pond in this volume see Chapter 6). Practitioners are almost conditioned to develop their skills in assessment in order to understand the complexities of a situation and build relationships to implement appropriate support. At the same time social workers are regularly and publicly criticised and vilified for failing to act quickly enough to prevent serious harm or even death of children. I agree completely with the supportive model as it is positive, optimistic and it encapsulates the beliefs, and motivations of those coming into the profession, that one can make a difference. I am however aware of the dangers of being too entrenched in the belief that people have the potential and capacity to change for the better and that people are intrinsically good, particularly when there are potential risks to children. With so much work being done to develop trusting relationships and promote positive change it can be difficult to make decisions to use powers that could potentially shatter those relationships and reverse any progress that may have already been made. Does one provide more support or use relevant powers, often against people's will, to provide protection? Feelings of helplessness and failure can be present if one cannot provide appropriate help. To make the right decision and to strike the right balance is the challenge all social workers face, but in my experience this can be achieved by working collectively with other professionals and trusting and valuing their opinion. More importantly, being open and trusting other professionals' opinion is crucial when making decisions. The alternative, decision making in isolation, could lead to dangerous situations or tragic consequences. I have regularly seen cases closed due to not meeting the criteria for assessment even though other professionals had asked for the case to remain open as they still had concerns. On one particular occasion I took a child to a police station after frequent attempts to request an assessment were refused and the child subsequently went in to foster care. On the other hand I have also been part of and have organised strategy meetings, which have led to thorough consideration of situations, informed and collective decisions being made and positive outcomes as a result.

Challenging stigma – raising profile and awareness

As mentioned earlier, to have a social worker employed by a school is still relatively uncommon. Therefore, in practice, other professionals, parents and children perceive the role, duties and responsibilities of the practitioner in many different ways. As a social worker in a school it is important to establish the role and raise the profile within the school community. In order to do this positively, one of the first and ongoing challenges is to address the stigma surrounding the profession of social work. The title of social worker evokes different responses from different people but the common response is generally negative. Many people, even other professionals, can view social workers as interfering busy bodies that take children away from their families. While this view, to some extent, is correct, in that social workers are indeed required by law to take action if they have concerns about the care and safety of children, it is the generalised assertion that is misplaced. Some people will inevitably view this as interference but what is often overlooked is the intentions to promote the well being of and protect the most vulnerable people in society from harm. Furthermore, people who train to become social workers are usually people who want to help others. I have experienced this type of negative view on more than one occasion and an example of this was during a telephone conversation. I was speaking to another agency and was asking to speak to a particular person. Asked who I was and what the call was regarding. I explained that I was a school social worker and was interrupted with 'social worker, in a school? Oh those poor children'. I then felt compelled to explain that I was actually trying to prevent some children from being evicted from their home and outline the role in more detail. Following this I had a different response of 'I didn't realise you social workers did that kind of thing, let me try and get hold of them for you'.

I often come across other generalisations made about the profession of social work such as, social workers are always late, they don't call you back, they don't share information and they don't act quickly enough. As a social worker I believe it is possible to challenge some of the commonly held perceptions through the actions and interactions the practitioner has on a daily basis. Moreover, in a school it is crucial to break down any barriers created by the negative perceptions of social work in order to carry out the work effectively and for people to feel comfortable enough to approach and seek help, support or advice. In a statutory setting assessments are carried out under section 17 and 47 of the *Children Act 1989* and social workers are required to become involved in a family's life. However, in a school, assessments are less formal and are carried out on a consensual basis. So unless the safety of a child is in question, the family has much more power to decide if they want involvement from the school social worker or not. Therefore in such a situation it is important to minimise potential barriers to effective communication and engagement. Being based in a school creates one of the best opportunities to carry out what is considered one of the key tasks of social work, namely preventative work. As a school social worker one is more accessible to both children and their parents and, if the practitioner is visible, contact occurs on a daily basis. The myriad of informal conversations that takes place in the playground with children and their parents are crucial for developing the positive relationships and breaking down the barriers within the school community. It is important to take every opportunity to speak to parents and tell them about the types of support provided by the school so that one is visible and approachable. Also, parents (school community) respond better when if there is an open door policy and that no problem is too big or too small or too trivial to be brought to ones attention. In practice this means making oneself available and being flexible in ones approach. On many occasions I had prioritised my work for the day when unexpectedly a parent will drop in because they want to talk. If possible (as I always try to do) I will rearrange my work and meet with the parent there and then. Many of these spontaneous encounters occur because the parent is facing a crisis or needs some form of help, support or advice. These impromptu meetings often lead to various types of immediate support and interventions being put in place to resolve the issues and prevent the situation from worsening. This type of approach is not something all agencies are able to offer. Social workers working with children and families often experience a high case load and complain that the bureaucracy involved in their work prevents them from spending time with service users. Time constraints or agency criteria and thresholds also impact on practitioners' ability to provide services to those families who are assessed as having less of a need compared to others. It is absolutely vital to efficiently manage the resources available within social care teams and apply resourses to those in most need of the service. However, this can decrease accessibility and can create a potential for the negative circumstances of children to escalate or for children to 'fall through the cracks' unless they are picked up by other services. Working with an open door policy can give people a positive experience of asking for and receiving help, which in turn means they may be more likely to seek out and engage with services in the future. It enables the practitioner to catch problems early, and through the development of positive relationships, provide informal and formal support over a long period of time in order to promote change. This approach also utilises one of the most powerful tools available when trying to engage with the whole school community, which is word of mouth (snowballing). People informing others about the help and support they had received goes a long way in changing peoples' negative perceptions of social work, though they do make the distinction between a school social worker and a social worker in the fieldwork.

Conclusion

One of the key points this chapter has tried to explore is the nature of social work practise in a school setting. I have tried to suggest that while there is a great deal of similarity in the types of problems LA and school social workers encounter there are also clear differences in the way they are able to approach their work and the level of power they are able to exercise. The ethos of the organisation, agency thresholds, the level of support given to practitioners, stigma, caseloads and many other factors that have been explored in this chapter can influence how effectively decisions are made and the type of service that is provided. Whilst policy underpins the profession as a whole, institutions can also shape the way social work is delivered. These influences can lead to a good quality service being provided resulting in positive outcomes for individuals and families. Equally, these influences can also lead to the erosion of the fundamental values that underpin the profession of social work, they can inhibit practitioners' ability to help people and the essence or nature of the work can potentially be lost along the way. The balancing act between managing resources, using relevant powers and providing support throws up many dilemmas and the challenge for all social workers and local authorities is to effectively manage Social Services in general and make the right decisions at the right time.

I have also tried to show that early intervention services and in particular the practise of social work in a school setting is crucial in order to counter the negative effects and adverse social and familial circumstances can have on a developing child. If the work is carried out effectively and informed decisions are made collectively, it is possible to increase the opportunities for children and support them to achieve their full potential. The broad range and contrast of work that is undertaken as a school social worker can be challenging but very rewarding and comes with an element of freedom with regards to the development of the role, how the work is prioritised and the types of work that are carried out. It also allows one to be creative in determining how support is delivered to individuals, families and the wider community.

References

Blyth, E. and Milner, J. (1997) *Social Work with Children: The Educational Perspective*

HMSO (1989) *The Children Act 1989*. London, HMSO.

HMSO (2002) *Education Act 2002*. London, HMSO.

HMSO (2003) *Every Child Matters*. London, HMSO.

HMSO (2004) *The Children Act 2004*. London, HMSO.

HMSO (2006) *Working Together to Safeguard Children: A guide to inter-agency working to safeguard and promote the welfare of children*. London, HMSO.

HMSO (2010) *Working Together to Safeguard Children: A guide to inter-agency working to safeguard and promote the welfare of children London*, HMSO.

Webb, R. (1994) *After the Deluge: Changing Roles and Responsibilities in the Primary School. Final Report of Research commissioned by the Association of Teachers and Lecturers.* London: Association of Teachers and Lecturers.

Website for Image:www.staffordshirechildrenstrust.org.uk

CHAPTER 9

Social Workers and the Courts

Akidi Ocan

Introduction

In this chapter I will address the reluctance of social workers to use the Family Courts and the full range of their statutory powers in their efforts to safeguard children. Social workers need to have a comprehensive knowledge of the extent of their powers and duties. They must also understand what is considered to be a lawful exercise of discretion and how and why the exercise of discretion might be challenged in judicial review proceedings.

The authority or power that the social worker can obtain from a court is likely to be a vital step towards securing the safety of a child even while further engagement with the family is still proposed. These powers are just as much a part of social worker's toolkit as their other professional expertise and they therefore need to have confidence in using the court processes to achieve preferred outcomes. Those outcomes properly include offering transparency so that children and their families know what the local authority's expectations are and exactly what powers are held by the local authority and the limits to be placed on their own roles.

The court arena is likely to be overwhelming for the children and families concerned and part of the role of the social worker is to help address the unfamiliarity and fears that they may have of the process to make it a more positive experience for the families and children. Perhaps understandably, social workers may also find the court arena daunting. When working with families, social workers are the 'experts' and the family is subjected to intense scrutiny, whereas when they are in court it is the content and quality of the social worker's professional work that is subject to critical examination giving the social worker the sense that they are 'on trial'. The social worker in court is not only expected to account for their own work but also for the overall performance, policies and funding decisions of their employer, the local social services authority. Contrast this with the freedom and self-assurance of the children's guardian who acts in an independent professional role and is not bound by an obligation to represent an employer, although they too are part of a wider organisation.

Different skills and abilities are required to prepare applications to court and the supporting evidence. Also the skills required to give oral evidence effectively and to deal with difficult cross-examination differ, for example, to that required of a social worker making a presentation in a meeting or to a panel. Whilst in court the social worker also has the burden of demonstrating to the court that they are an expert in the process so that the evidence is given equal weight with the evidence of the children's guardian, and even the Consultant Psychiatrist or other experts in the proceedings.

Greater attention ought to be paid to equipping social workers with the expertise necessary to undertake their role through specific training and familiarisation activities. In this Chapter I will set out what social workers will need to be familiar with if they are to make optimum use of the court arena as an indispensable safeguarding tool for the children to whom they owe a duty.

The social workers powers under the *Children Act*

The task of the social worker when working with children and families is without doubt a complex one and for the social worker to perform their role in a correct manner, a comprehensive understanding of child protection legislation is essential. This includes the ethos of the Acts, Regulations and Guidance and the context in which they were introduced.

The *Children Act 1989* recognised the primary role of the parent in the satisfactory development of a child. The legislation appreciates that there is a balance between safety and risk: a child can be raised in a risk free environment but lose the love and individual nurturing that only a parent can offer, providing the child with the emotional security and feelings of positive self worth. Conversely, the effort to maintain the child within the family unit could tip the scales too far leaving the child exposed to harm from which he or she may struggle to recover. It is therefore imperative for social workers to remain conscious at all times of the principle that working in partnership with parents and families is encouraged but only if and to the extent that such work promotes the child's safety, security and wellbeing.

The circumstances of a child in need may give rise to concerns about their safety and welfare or a child at risk of harm may also have needs that should be assessed and provided for under section 17. The social worker may have come into the family by one route but this does not mean that they can not see and act on what they would have seen if they had come in by the other route. It is as well that the social worker strives to keep the full range of statutory functions in the forefront of their minds so as to avoid missing something that may be crucial to the welfare of that child.

Seeking the voluntary engagement of the parents is widely accepted as the appropriate way to proceed and, provided that engagement is achieving the desired outcomes for the child and unacceptable risks are effectively managed, securing a safer and more nurturing home environment for the child through the agreement, understanding and development of the parents is unarguably the best outcome.

Now more than ever, statutory and other formal processes encourage partnership working between parents, the wider family and a range of professional agencies including social services, health services, education and the police. So far as the parents and families were concerned, there was a need to redress the balance of power and in the two decades since the 1989 Act was implemented social workers have become comfortable with that acknowledgment of the central role that the parents play. However, the law is unambiguous; the welfare of the child is 'the court's paramount consideration' *Children Act 1989* (section1 (1)) and as such it must be the local authority's first consideration.

In fact social workers can only intervene in families further to the local social services statutory functions and the duties and powers provided in the body of legislation that governs their role. The local authority's social work service performs the functions assigned by the *Local Authority Social Services Act 1970*. Were it not for the assignment of those functions, any intervention could be argued to be a breach of the family's human right to privacy (ECHR, 1950). To be fair to the parents, it is clear that the playing field must level; in other words they must be armed with all of the information that will be presented against them. It would be unfair to base a decision on a fact or a suspicion that has not been clearly articulated. But unfortunately, this is the type of error that can be easy to fall into when the social worker, even to spare the parents feelings, fail to be straight about what is going wrong and skirts round the edges of the issue.

The social worker must ask themselves the question, what is my specific statutory function here and what powers and duties have I been given to perform my role? So for example, do I have concerns about this child because she or he is a child in need (*Children Act 1989*b) or do I have concerns about his or her safety (*Children Act 1989*c) or both. This question can only be answered by assessment.

The Public Law Outline

This approach is enshrined in the Public Law Outline (PLO) introduced in 2008, which requires an initial assessment to be undertaken followed by a core assessment whether the social worker has before them a child who is thought to be a child in need or a child at risk of harm. The core assessment will determine whether the child is in fact in need or at risk or both and what to do next. The PLO prescribes that the social worker commission any specialist assessment that may be required, set up Family Meetings/ Family Group Conferences where these are thought to be relevant and plan for the child's future care which must include consideration of placement/permanence options. (Ref: The Public Law Outline). If the Core Assessment determines that the child is in need, a Child in Need Plan and services must then be decided on and provided and arrangements should be made for periodic reviews of the plan and services. If there are safeguarding concerns the PLO lays down that the route to follow is a strategy discussion, followed by section 47 enquiries and that the Core Assessment should be started. This is then to be followed by a Child Protection Conference, the formulation of a Child Protection Plan and the completion of the Core Assessment. The Core Assessment is discussed in the Core Group and the process is then completed in a Child Protection Review conference, which records any resulting revised Child Protection Plan (*Public Law Outline*, 2010).

The PLO has levelled the playing field for parents more than ever before. A legal planning meeting involving the parents and their legal advisors together with the local authority must be held to agree further action to safeguard the child. That meeting and most importantly the requirement to issue the parent with a letter before proceedings is an acknowledgement that fairness dictates that parents must be in possession of all of the information that the local authority has taken into account in concluding that the level of risk to which the child is exposed is unacceptable. The parent is represented at the legal planning meeting and it is expected that the parent will be given every opportunity to engage in the process in partnership with relevant statutory agencies. The only ground on which full and complete disclosure would not be justified is to prevent further harm or immediate harm to the child. A parent who does not make the required changes may ultimately relinquish their right to exercise their parental responsibility for the child, provided they have been given a reasonable amount of support and the opportunity to make appropriate changes. Social workers are not being asked to judge parents in a moral sense. Not all parents who are relieved of the right to exercise parental responsibility are culpable; it is not a moral judgement on them. Rather, it is an acceptance that, even with the support, encouragement and assistance available to them, they are not able to ensure that the child is kept safe and secure and adequately nurtured.

Where the measures set out in the letter before proceedings do not achieve the desired outcome, either because the meeting is not successful or because the plan is not adequately protecting the child, proceedings may be commenced. It is central to the PLO that if the concerns should reach the threshold for a care or supervision order, an application must be made. Alternatively, the meeting could decide to issue a letter before proceedings the format for which is prescribed in the PLO.

The most liberating aspect for the social worker in the world of safeguarding children is that the social worker does not shoulder the burden of deciding whether the threshold has been reached for such an application to be made. The social work manager, and the legal adviser and other partner agencies play a crucial part in the decision making process so that the social worker should feel confident that the right assessment of threshold is made. An application to remove a child from their parent's care is a serious step and it is one that is not taken lightly by any of the parties involved. The local authority's legal representative will base their opinions on the merits of an application on the evidence presented to them that may point to the likelihood that the child is suffering or will suffer significant harm. If there is little in the Core Assessment to support the social worker's concerns, it is probable that the legal representative will be concerned that the evidence does not confirm that the threshold for proceedings has been met and that proceedings cannot be justified in the circumstances. Also, it is as well to remember that the more thorough an assessment, the more likely it is that the right decision will be made and that it will be robust and stand up to whatever scrutiny it is subjected to within the proceedings.

The Initial Assessment provides a summary of the work undertaken by children's services in collaboration with other agencies and although the Initial Assessment will of necessity be brief in that it must be completed within a short period (seven days), it must be a thorough and carefully recorded piece of work. It is the first opportunity to flag up any harm that the child is suffering or is likely to suffer due to shortcomings in their parenting. Even at the Initial Assessment stage the child must be seen and communicated with in an age appropriate way. On any view of the child protection tragedies that have occurred in our time, the child not being seen should be considered a red marker warning. If unable to gain access to the child the social worker must apply for an order from the court unless they are satisfied that the child's welfare can be guaranteed without an order. The case of Baby P illustrates that being seen in the literal sense of the word may not be enough and a social worker must be alert to methods a parent may use to hide indicators of abuse (see Chapter 5 of this volume).

The parents must be asked for their consent to contact other relevant agencies unless the seeking of consent would in itself place the child at risk. A child with sufficient understanding and capacity also has a right to give consent for information to be sought. If refused by the parent, that refusal must be the subject of further consideration and thought must be given to whether an application should be made to a court for authority to obtain the information in spite of the parent's refusal of consent. Analysis of the work completed for the Initial Assessment is not just a formality but it ensures that the right decisions are being recorded and that any further actions and the Initial Plan that may be agreed make a real difference to the outcomes for the child.

A Core Assessment will be a more detailed assessment since further time is allowed. Detail and evidence based assessment is key and only a thorough piece of work will enable the correct decisions to be made. Without a comprehensive Core Assessment containing a risk assessment and risk management strategy, the social worker could not begin to truly work in partnership with the parents and family and with other relevant agencies to safeguard a child. The Core Assessment is the professional evidence based evaluation of the likely harms that may befall the child should there be no change in the environment and parenting that the child is receiving. At the outset all likely harms are to be identified and enumerated without regard to whether they are sufficiently significant to meet the threshold for proceedings. The family's ability to meet the child's needs must be specifically addressed in the assessment.

The social worker must have as accurate a picture as possible of what is going on and what that means for the child. This is not only gained from the partner agencies such as schools or health services but also from the parents. The social worker must find a way to build rapport with the family in order to gain accurate information from them and offer them support and reassurance throughout the process. Undoubtedly, one of the greatest professional challenges for a social worker in children's services must be establishing that rapport whilst recognising that the parent may be manipulative or untruthful. Undertaking the assessment is itself challenging. The social worker must meet the required timescales whilst gathering and double checking from various sources the information that is being drawn together whilst keeping the parent in the picture and ensuring that the child remains safe whilst this work in ongoing. However, without a full and true picture, a social worker could not honestly and openly inform the parents of the areas of concern or how the local authority would expect to see their concerns addressed in order to be satisfied that the child is not at risk of significant harm.

Use of the court

The local authority applies for an order depending on the steps that it may believe are essential to secure the child's welfare and these can range from child assessment orders (*Children Act 1989d*) emergency protection orders (*Children Act 1989e*) and care or supervision orders (*Children Act 1989f*) to orders that prevent contact with the child by persons who pose risks to them (*Children Act 1989g*) or enable children who are missing to be recovered (*Children Act 1989h*). Orders may be interim or final and may be sought on an emergency basis.

A social worker must expect that any assessment will be disclosed in the process of the application and the court's trust and confidence in the social worker's factual evidence and recommendations to the court will begin to be formed from reading all of the relevant documentation. If the Initial Assessment or the Core Assessment is a flimsy incomplete piece of work, this will not assist in building that confidence.

Where the social worker can also make a difference to the family of the child is by offering support and guidance for them through a process that will naturally seem formal and daunting whether or not they have had any previous experience of it. In order to do this effectively the social worker must have a good knowledge of what the process is and how it will work in relation to the family before them. The parent needs to be fully informed from the outset that the Initial Assessment and a Core Assessment that are being completed may later lead to a decision to proceed to court.

The social worker can gain confidence from the knowledge that when considering whether or not to make an order or orders under the *Children Act 1989* the court cannot do so unless it considers that making that order is better for the child than making no order at all (*Children Act 1989i*). Nothing is taken for granted. Not only must the harm suffered or the likely harm be proved to the courts satisfaction but the manner of response must be shown to be effective and necessary and in the best interests of the child. Obtaining an order from the court is neither to be seen as a success nor a failure of partnership working. A court order is nothing more than the authority of the court to take certain measures and it is therefore a route to achieving the preferred outcome for the child.

The Family Courts are just as much an arena for social work professional practise as the various panels, multi agency meetings and the service user's home is likely to be. The court may well be an unfamiliar environment for many but it is one that the social worker must get to grips with in order to practise as a professional in the field of children's social work. If it remains an unknown with the inevitable anxiety and fear of going into the unknown, it presents a blockage in that for many there will always be a natural reticence to venture into the court arena. The aim of any effective social worker must be to be as adept at using the court process as the independent expert or legal professionals.

On entry into the profession of social work, the novice is recommended to take every opportunity to familiarise themselves not only with the range of applications they could make to safeguard a child, but also to develop an understanding of the type of evidence that would persuade a court that the criteria are met to justify the making of the order sought.

Taking time to understand what the Family Court is, its role, and the location of the courts that they are most likely to be using and who are going to be the decision makers in those courts is time well spent. All this ought to be done before the social worker is faced with making a particular application and in fact some of this work should ideally be included into a social worker's induction programme.

The social worker must understand the roles of the various people who will be in that courtroom with them. This is especially useful in preparation for giving evidence. Everyone in that courtroom is there to perform a different task and for a particular purpose and function. Knowing what their reason for being there is will help the social worker to anticipate what they are going to do or say in that role.

The District Judge is, of course, the decision maker. The questions that come from the

District Judge will be directed towards the single purpose of enabling the decision maker to make the difficult decisions in a lawful way. They are charged with the responsibility of determining facts, considering risks to the child and ultimately deciding whether the criteria are met to support the making of an order bearing in mind the no order principle.

The legal representatives need to be looked at and considered separately. Who represents the mother? Who represents the father? What is the parent's response to the application, are they in agreement with each other or are they competing. Do they accept the concerns of the professionals or do they contest the facts. What is their response to the proposed care plan? All of this will be evident in advance from their responses to the application and the written evidence they have provided. Similarly for the child's solicitor, what does their report recommend, do they take issue with the local authority's case and if so, on what points. This information will guide the social workers preparation for responding to questions.

For the social worker in court, detailed and thorough preparation is the key. It will enable the social worker to demonstrate their professionalism and their command of their own professional field of expertise. The social worker in most cases will have had the opportunity to rehearse their own evidence in that the statement that they have prepared is a summary of the evidence that they are going to give orally. The more thought and consideration the social worker puts into their own statement, the more prepared they will be to explain their assessments, conclusions and recommendations to the court. A carefully thought through statement that sets out the factual evidence that supports the decision making and then goes on to analyse those facts and explain the conclusions is what the court is looking to see. The best statements will anticipate the questions that will be going through the decision makers mind and answer them. This is not difficult to do given that the welfare checklist helpfully sets out what the court will have regard to in reaching its decision (*Children Act 1989*).

Having a thorough knowledge of the children's services entire file, even when the social worker has been allocated to the case after the proceedings have commenced, flagging up the significant entries in preparation for giving evidence so that relevant events can be found easily whilst they are in the witness box, taking the files to court so that the records are on hand all ensures that the social worker is thoroughly prepared to undertake the task ahead.

One of the trickiest aspects for the social worker giving evidence is to accept that they perform a multiple role within the courtroom. On the one hand the social worker is a professional holding their personal views and opinions that are formed following their own assessment and consideration of the circumstances of the child and family. These views are then taken to a Legal Planning Meeting where there is a joint consideration of whether the threshold for proceedings is met. The social worker may find that they do not fully agree with the conclusion but if it is decided to proceed to issue, it is the social worker that is called upon to represent the local authority's position in court as an officer of the council to whom the task has been delegated. This can also arise where the local authority's policy is for a particular course of action. The social worker may find that he or she is under cross-examination being pressed to explain a position that they did not personally support. The social worker may find themselves being asked the direct question, 'do you agree with this action' and if the question is put they will need to find a truthful way to respond that is concordant with their dual roles as representing the authority and remaining true to their professional opinion. Generally it is not impossible to predict when this type of dilemma is likely to arise because, in the lead in time, the social worker will have a warning as to where their own views and those of their employer may diverge. This can be discussed with line managers and the legal advisers and a form of words can be agreed in advance which should assist an answer to be given to this type of question.

The social worker must be aware of the various possible options that enable challenges to be made to their decision-making. In addition to the statutory complaints process and complaints to the Local Government Ombudsman, a judicial review can be sought. Where it is possible to make a decision between different courses of action and the local authority chooses one route as opposed to another in accordance with its 'policy', the route chosen may be challenged using the legal process known as judicial review. This is an opportunity for the High Court to consider the decision and the policy and to consider its lawfulness against a number of specified criteria including the lawfulness and reasonableness of the decision and the policy. Where the local authority is given discretion to exercise it must always do so. In other words, where it is required to choose between different courses of action, the local authority cannot say that it declines to make a decision or it cannot have a policy that says it will always make that decision in a predetermined way. If it did so, it would be successfully challenged for fettering its discretion and this will always be unlawful.

The word 'cross-examination' can be enough in itself to drive a fear in to the heart of a witness. It brings with it the natural irritation that some have at being contradicted or undermined or simply being called upon to account for ones actions. It is important to understand and be familiar with the fact that in a court arena a completely different convention applies. The verbal exchange between counsel and the witness is not a conversation. Counsel asks a question of the witness and the witness delivers the response not to counsel as they would in a normal conversation, but to the decision maker in the courtroom. For example, it is not considered to be impolite for the witness to look at the questioner to hear or receive the question and then turn and face the decision maker to deliver the response to that question. In fact, the witness who uses this technique is immediately marked out as a professional person who is experienced in the conventions of the courtroom to those who are regularly in court in their professional lives.

In everyday life when a person gives an account of an incident and they are told that a different version of the incident is true, this is tantamount to saying that the first account was a lie. In court, counsel asks a question of a witness firstly to put their client's case so the question is their way of saying that their client has a different recollection or account of an event. If they fail to put their clients account through the cross examination, the decision maker automatically accepts the witnesses version of the incident as being true as it went unchallenged. When the social worker is preparing for cross examination, they must therefore trawl though the statements and reports filed by the other parties to see where there are factual disagreements because they can then identify all of the questions that will be put to them in cross examination.

So, for example, the social workers evidence is that the father did not attend a prearranged supervised contact visit and he gave no prior notice that he was not coming. The children were disappointed. Father's legal representative says that father telephoned the contact centre to say that his car broke down on the way and that he could not get there in time. The witness will be asked whether it is correct that father left a message with the contact centre to say that he was late because his car broke down. If the witness did not receive such a message he need only say that he did not receive such a message and that he checked at the reception desk several times and was told that there were no messages from the father. It is possible that both accounts are true and that a message was left but it was not handed over to the relevant person so the children were disappointed. Father still has to prove that he left the message.

The tone of voice that the legal representative may use in putting the question can be quite unnerving for some but the witness need only focus on telling the truth of what they do know and being clear to the court when something is put to them that they do not know the answer to and why.

The witness is cross examined in turn by the legal representatives for each of the parties present in court and the decision maker may ask a question or two to seek clarification on a point. However, at the start, through examination in chief and at the end of the social worker's evidence, through re-examination, the legal representatives representing the local authority ask them questions. This gives a chance for the social worker to set out their own account. In examination in chief, the witness cannot be asked questions with yes or no answers. So, for example, the witness will not be asked 'did you check at the reception desk for messages when father did not arrive?' Rather the question will be 'when father did not arrive for contact, what did you do?' Answer, 'I checked at the reception desk for messages'. Re-examination focuses on allowing the witness to clarify or respond to issues that have come up in cross-examination.

Once the fact finding stage of the hearing has been determined, the court moves on to the stage of deciding what is to happen to the child and the local authorities proposed care plan for the child will come under scrutiny (*Children Act 1989k*). If the preparation of the plan has been sound with and is underpinned by thorough assessment and determination of the needs of the child, and proper attention paid to the range of alternatives for meeting the needs of the child, the social worker can demonstrate in their evidence their belief in the local authorities plan. This is where a social worker who is confident in the proposed plan has the advantage over one who may struggle with a policy that they cannot support for instance because a course of action is not recommended to the court due to the cost implications for the authority. Professional challenges to the care plan from the children's guardian or other expert witnesses can best be tackled when they are anticipated and prepared for. The objective of the Issues Resolution Hearing is to resolve and narrow issues and identify key remaining issues requiring resolution. By working through the other parties case summaries, the parties witness statements, the threshold documents, and the Case Analysis and Recommendations, the social worker ought to develop a good understanding of the areas that his or her preparation needs to be focused on. There will be an Issues Resolution Hearing before the final hearing 'to resolve and narrow issues' and 'to identify any remaining key issues' (*Practice Direction Public Law*, 2010) which should leave the social worker in absolutely no doubt prior to the final hearing where they must concentrate their efforts in preparing to give evidence.

With everything that the social worker must consider, one very positive aspect of the court process that may be overlooked is that the court is the final arbiter and so the ultimate decisions about whether a child remains living within their family or whether contact with the family is to continue is not a burden that the social worker carries themselves. Having presented the application and evidence, the court makes the determination and the court will not automatically adopt the social worker's recommendations but will analyse and test these to be sure before making the order asked for. Provided the family has had an opportunity to take part fully and equally in the process, they may also be helped to come to terms with the final outcome. These are factors that should offer the social work practitioner confidence to explore the full range of options that may be available to them where the responsibility for protecting a child from harm falls to them.

References

Council of Europe (1950) *European Convention for the Protection of Human Rights and Fundamental Freedoms* (Article 8). Rome, Council of Europe.
HMSO (1989a) *Children Act 1989* (section1 (1)). London, HMSO.
HMSO (1989b) *Children Act 1989* (section 17). London, HMSO.

HMSO (1989c) *Children Act 1989* (section 47). London, HMSO.

HMSO (1989d) *Children Act 1989* (section 43). London, HMSO.

HMSO (1989e) *Children Act 1989* (section 44). London, HMSO.

HMSO (1989f) *Children Act 1989* (section 31). London, HMSO.

HMSO (1989g) *Children Act 1989* (section 8). London, HMSO.

HMSO (1989h) *Children Act 1989* (section 50). London, HMSO.

HMSO (1989i) *Children Act 1989* (section1 (5)). London, HMSO.

HMSO (1989j) *Children Act 1989* (section1 (3)). London, HMSO.

HMSO (1989k) *Children Act 1989* (section 31A). London, HMSO.

Ministry of Justice (2008) *The Public Law Outline.* London, Ministry of Justice.

Ministry of Justice (2010) *Practice Direction Public Law Proceedings Guide to Case Management* London, Ministry of Justice.

CHAPTER 10

Critical Reflection and Power in Social Work

Jan Fook

Introduction

A central argument of this book is that power, both how the concept is understood and how it actually operates in the practice of social work, is complex and fraught with tensions. It is particularly problematic if power is conceptualised in too simplistic a manner, which does not match how it might be experienced by the many different parties involved in the practice of social work.

Critical reflection on practice is a process which can unearth many different disjunctures between theoretical conceptualisations of practice, and the particular assumptions embedded in what actually happens. The process can therefore be useful in revealing these more hidden understandings of power, as evidenced in everyday practice. In turn, awareness of these hidden conceptualisations can be useful in crafting a more complex understanding of power, and hence a more sophisticated and responsive set of practices.

This chapter aims to illustrate how critical reflection on assumptions about power (as embedded in the everyday practice of workers) can help forge a more complex and responsive practice. It will begin with a brief introduction to the theory and practice of critical reflection, particularly the notion of unearthing assumptions. This section will also include the theory of power included in this particular approach to critical reflection. There will be some brief coverage of the sorts of assumptions about power which are common in social work thinking, and then close with an outline how these conceptions of power might be reworked in a more complex way, through a critical reflection process.

An introduction to the critical reflection process

What is critical reflection? The idea of reflection, in more recent times, is generally attributed to Dewey (1933) and refers to the process whereby people learn from experience. It involves

126

examining thinking for its underlying foundations and implications and may also extend to the emotional aspects of experience (Boud et al., 1985). However not all reflection is necessarily critical. 'Critical' may refer to deep levels of reflection, which examine the fundamental bases of thinking. It may also refer to reflection which uses a 'critical' theoretical framework to expose thinking which performs political functions. We will explore this latter meaning in more detail in the following section.

Clearly there are many different ways of learning from experience, and therefore many different ways of reflecting. Donald Schon's concept of reflective practice (1983) is perhaps the most well-known in professional learning circles. It rests upon the idea that there are often large gaps between what professionals espouse (say or think) they do, and what is actually implied by what they do. Lack of awareness of this, or an inability to make the espoused theory match the actual practice, may contribute to ineffective practice, or an inability to change or improve it. Schon's model therefore involves unearthing the assumptions involved in actual practice, so that professionals might become more aware of the gaps, and how they might move to close them (and thus improve their practice).

Schon's model is excellent for outlining a practical process for examining the basic assumptions underlying our thinking and practice. What it is not so good at is providing a theoretical framework for guiding what we look at, why, and how we might evaluate the appropriateness of these. Many different frameworks may be used for doing this. In my model I use a number of theoretical concepts and perspectives to do this: namely reflexivity, postmodernism/deconstruction, and critical theory. I will develop these in more detail in the following section, particularly how they relate to concepts of power.

However in this section I will outline the practical process of critical reflection, as a process for learning from professional experience, based primarily on Schon's approach of unearthing hidden assumptions. The critical reflection normally takes place in a small group (facilitated by a designated facilitator) in which each of the participants takes a turn to reflect, assisted by the other group members as peers. Each participant brings an example of a concrete piece of their own experience, which has a direct bearing on their learning about professional practice. This example is normally written in the form of a critical (significant) incident, which the person has prepared beforehand, and chosen using specific guidelines. The group helps each person critically reflect, using questions (derived from several different frameworks) which are designed to help elicit underlying assumptions. The group also agrees to support a learning climate conducive to reflection, one which encourages acceptance of each person's perspective enough to allow them to challenge (for themselves) whatever might be taken for granted in it.

This process takes place in two main stages: the first focuses on unearthing assumptions; and the second focuses on the changed thinking and actions which arise from an awareness of these assumptions. It is important that the reflection is structured in two stages, and that the work of each stage is kept separate. The first stage is important for simply accessing the underlying thinking (without necessarily having to pass judgement on it) simply in order to expose thinking so that there is an opportunity to evaluate it. It is important that this hidden thinking is evaluated by the person reflecting, rather than having evaluations imposed by other group members. Often the person reflecting is able to evaluate their hidden thinking almost naturally, in that once it is exposed and spoken, there may be obvious discrepancies which seem inappropriate in current contexts. It is important however that the process occurs so that group members can discover this for themselves. It is also important in this stage that there is no pressure to 'find solutions' or to be able to work out what to do. Such pressure can inhibit a person's openness to finding new ways of seeing things.

At the end of this first stage of reflection each person should have been able to unearth some fairly deep assumptions which they may wish to re-scrutinise in the light of their current experience or other thinking. Sometimes this scrutiny may result in wanting to change the thinking which has been unearthed, or sometimes the person may wish to reaffirm this fundamental thinking, and readjust their current practice or thinking accordingly. Each person may undertake several different permutations of these changes, and in relation to several different sets of assumptions as well. In any case, they will take some new thinking away from the first session, and this new thinking will form the basis of their reflections for the second stage.

In preparation for the second stage, each participant is asked:

- To restate the fundamental thinking that was unearthed.
- What changes (in thinking and practice) may result from this.
- To try to reformulate (or put a label on) their changed thinking (and practice).

In the actual group discussion in the second stage, group members assist each person further with each of these aspects. What each person ends up with (at the end of the second stage) is a reformulated principle which they hope will guide their practice.

There are many different ways to theorise this process. If we think of it as learning from experience, then what each participant has been enabled to do is to devise new guidelines for action, based on an examination of the deep thinking underlying their past experiences. Sometimes I have referred to the process as one of deconstruction (stage 1) and reconstruction (stage 2) (Fook, 2002). It can also be seen as a process of creating practice theory or knowledge, directly from practice experience, (Fook, 2008: viii).

Barbara's example

Following is a specific example, which will help illustrate the kinds of changes which can take place in the process. Barbara (a social worker and middle manager in a large national government bureaucracy) participated in critical reflection training over a period of some months. The *critical incident* she brought actually occurred in her personal life, when she was travelling in Ireland with her husband (both Barbara and her husband lived in Australia). They had planned to meet up with a large number of their Irish relatives at a hotel, only to find when they arrived that there were not enough rooms booked. This led to an altercation between Barbara's husband and the hotel manager. The critical incident for Barbara was when she physically stepped between the two men to stop the argument. The incident was 'critical' for Barbara because she 'Didn't want to be a "control freak"' (her words).

In discussion with the group what emerged were her assumptions about control; about someone always needing to be in control, and the idea that Barbara equated control with the need for action. She reflected further on what might be underlying these assumptions, and surfaced her own needs to be in control. She then realised how her assumptions about good professional practice equated it with the need to take action. A fundamental assumption of hers was that a good professional was one who was in control by taking action.

When she reflected further on this however she realised that she 'Didn't want to be a "control freak"' and wondered whether these assumptions about control might be based on her own 'fear of uncertainty'? This was the end of Barbara's stage one reflections.

However she continued to reflect after this group session, and some weeks later both her emotions and her assumptions came together in an experience she had. She caught herself telling a staff member (who she was trying to motivate to implement a new program) that he needed to 'stay with the uncertainty . . .'

This experience was critical for Barbara in that she realised she was telling him to do the very thing which she was concerned about, but about which she had obviously formed some new ideas. In stage two therefore she decided that she needed to reconstruct her desired practice as 'being powerful in uncertainty' or 'structured uncertainty'. This was her new label for her practice, or her new guiding principle. When the group asked how she would do this, she spoke of creating her own 'emotional scaffolding' to help her in new situations. This 'scaffolding' would be made up of her store of knowledge or skills which she had amassed from learning to work in other new situations in the past. She would use knowledge of these skills to bolster her confidence on entering yet other new situations.

In summary, the critical reflection process for Barbara involved her moving from a fundamental assumption (and emotion) about a 'fear of uncertainty' to a new guiding principle about 'power in uncertainty'. She has learnt from her experience by deconstructing it to reformulate (reconstruct) it in a new way. In the process she has also created her own particular practice theory ('power in uncertainty' or 'structured uncertainty').

The theory of power in critical reflection

As I mentioned above, I use several theoretical frameworks in my model to assist people in interpreting their experiences and analysing their assumptions, so that they can make their own judgements about whether and how they might want to change their assumptions or actions. Each of these frameworks (the concept of reflexivity, postmodernism/deconstruction and critical theory) has implications for an understanding of power. I will outline each of these in turn.

1. Reflexivity

The idea of reflexivity is often associated with social science research (Marcus, 1994) and in particular, fields like anthropology (for example, Rosaldo, 1993). In this respect, reflexivity is important in appreciating the affect that the researcher has upon what is being researched. For anthropologists studying 'foreign' cultures, this was particularly important in being able to identify the biases of their own cultures, so that they minimised their influence in interpreting others. In the health and social care professions reflexivity has been defined in various ways. Steier (1991) defines it as a 'turning back on itself'. White (2002: 10) emphasises the ability to look both inwards and outwards to recognise the connections with social and cultural understandings. This is similar to my own, which involves the ability to recognise that all aspects of ourselves and our contexts influence the way we research (or create knowledge) (Fook, 1999). I am using the idea of research here to refer to all the different ways in which we create knowledge – some occur on a more formal and systematic basis, yet others are used daily, and often in unarticulated ways to make sense of immediate surroundings. In this sense, research, or knowledge creation, is integral to the daily business of living.

Therefore, in order to be reflexive, we need to be aware of the many and varied ways in which we might create, or at least influence, the type of knowledge we use. This means that we also need to be aware of the various ways that we, as physical, emotional, biographically constructed, and social beings, might participate in creating our knowledge (and our idea of 'truth' or 'reality'). We might participate in creating or recognising knowledge in several different ways: for example, by filtering or selecting whatever information we believe to be relevant (this may depend, for example, on our age, gender, mood, the time of day) by using certain tools or frameworks which automatically filter or interpret information in certain ways (certain theoretical frameworks or perspectives have been popular at different times in history) or by being part of a culture or context in which only particular types of information are disseminated or accepted.

Reflexivity then, is integral to our understanding of the operation of power, in that power is integral to how and what knowledge is made and accepted. When we understand, by being reflexive, how we ourselves participate in creating and valuing or privileging certain types of knowledge, we also begin to understand what power we create and support, and what practices, structures and relations are in turn created and supported. Such a conception is vital in social work practice, as it is easy to distance ourselves from the sources of power, and to feel alienated from the possibility of making changes in our social environments. A reflexive way of seeing, used as a framework in a critical reflection process, can help directly connect individual thinking and actions as powerful influences, by drawing the links between how individual knowledge making is inextricably bound with social forces.

2. Postmodernism and deconstructionism

Postmodern and deconstructive thinking can help to extend our understanding of different perspectives on knowledge creation, and in some senses they provide some further theoretical backbone to the idea of reflexivity. By postmodernism, I am referring simply to the questioning of 'modernist' (or linear and unified) thinking (Parton, 1994). It represents a questioning of the idea that knowledge must be arrived at in a progressive or cumulative way, and that it is arrived at through consensus. Postmodern thinking alerts us to the relationship between knowledge and power (as does the notion of reflexivity). However the postmodern concept of discourse provides more substance to this thinking.

Discourses are, in simple terms, ways of communicating about a phenomenon. They focus on the role of language in forming our understanding of phenomena. The terms and phraseology we use to describe our experiences carry implicit assumptions about ourselves and our social world, and of course, about relative statuses and power. Whichever discourses are dominant usually points to which groups are in power ie. the discourses of the dominant groups usually are the ones more generally adopted, which then perpetuates the dominant group's privileged position. Dominant discourses usually determine what knowledge is counted as legitimate. The way we speak about things, what we choose to label and what is not labelled, and the relationships we imply through the language we use, all have a role in marking what is legitimate and what is thus powerful.

A particularly useful concept is that of dichotomous thinking, or binary opposites (Berlin, 1990). These are paired categories of phenomena that are total (refer to the whole population), mutually exclusive (one cannot be a member of both), binary (there are only two categories) and oppositional (the categories are defined against each other). The categories 'male' and 'female' are prime examples. 'Service user' and 'professional' is another. The concept of binary opposites often underlies how we make social difference, and is therefore a crucial part of identity-making, and by implication, inclusion and exclusion. For instance, we often attribute inferiority to the second part of a binary category (e.g. 'female' is inferior to 'male' by definition) and indeed the second part of the binary is often defined in terms of the first (e.g. females are defined as 'not male'). Thereby the first category in the binary opposite retains primacy. In this sense, the practice of creating and using binary opposites plays an important role in creating power differences and inequalities.

It is also useful to think about how we construct binary opposites in other areas of working or living, such as in creating forced choice scenarios, or dilemmas. I often encounter practitioners who feel they have reached an impasse in practice because they believe there is a fundamental dilemma or conflict involved. For example, social workers often concep-tualise a basic dilemma in their work as being between 'care' and 'control'; or about 'value-based practice' versus 'outcome-driven practice', as if the two categories are mutually exclusive. Postmodern thinking can lead us to question whether these divisions are the only way of thinking about a problem, leading us to speculate whether it might be possible that there are more than two categories. This opens the way to formulate more complex ways of working. For instance, much work might be about both 'care' and 'control' so that perhaps there is at least a third category, that of 'caring control'. This reformulation can lead to a different way of seeing practice, and provide a way forward in practice.

Postmodern and deconstructive thinking provides a useful framework for understanding the operation of power in critical reflection by showing how we can deconstruct our thinking in order to expose how we participate in constructing power. This opens the way for us to explore conflicts and contradictions which may have been previously silenced. This in turn allows us to build a more complex practice, which takes account of varying and differing perspectives, and in particular allows more marginal perspectives to be recognised and incorporated.

3. Critical social theory

Whilst postmodern thinking sheds light on how we participate in constructing power, critical social theory provides a framework to evaluate which forms of power and outcomes are desirable. What is critical social theory? Here I focus on the common themes, drawn from a range of authors (see Fook, 2002; Agger, 1998). Critical social theory recognises that power has both personal and structural aspects. Individuals often participate in their own domination, by holding self-defeating beliefs about their place in the social structure, their own power and possibilities for change. Social change, to be effective, must occur at both personal and collective levels. This involves recognising that knowledge often has an empirical 'reality', but the way that knowledge is used and interpreted may be constructed (socially and personally). Therefore, in bringing about social and personal change, communication and dialogue are important so that new shared understandings can be created.

Several of these key points are crucial to the practice of critical reflection. For instance, connecting personal experience and beliefs with structural arrangements, shows how our own personal assumptions may include an implicit aspect of power. Once these hidden ideas are exposed, people who hold them are thus given the power to change them (Fook and Askeland, 2006). Emphasising the dialogical element supports the social and collective aspect of critical reflection.

In summary then, power is theorised in different ways, and each of these has specific uses in a critical reflection process. The concept of reflexivity allows us to see the role of our own selves in constructing knowledge (and power); postmodern thinking provides specific substance by developing the role of language and discourse in this construction; and critical social theory emphasises the links between personal experience and collective constructions of power.

What assumptions about power emerge from social workers critically reflecting on their practice experience?

In this section I will analyse and summarise some of the main assumptions which social work practitioners make about power (as they emerge from their own accounts of their own practice). I draw on several key sources for this material (Napier and Fook, 2000; Fook, 2004; Fook and Askeland, 2006; Fook and Gardner, 2007, Ch. 8; Pockett and Giles, 2008). I have chosen to analyse this material as all involve accounts of actual practice experiences, and/or an evaluation of the changes in thinking which have taken place as a result of undertaking a process of critical reflection. It is useful to refer to these references to gain a sense of the broader range of changes which take place as a result of critical reflection. In this section I focus only on what underlying thinking has emerged regarding power. In the following section I will analyse and summarise the kinds of changes in thinking about power which have resulted from the critical reflection process.

There are four main types of assumptions about power which underlie practitioners' accounts of their practice:

1. Power and dichotomous thinking.
2. The power of theory.
3. Power and possibilities for change.
4. The power of discourse.

1. Power and dichotomous thinking

This type of thinking probably includes most of the assumptions regarding power. Some assumptions involve creating a simple binary opposite based on a 'powerful' vs 'powerless' dichotomy. This might take the form of dividing 'experts' from 'those to be empowered' (Shipway, 2000) or more obviously, 'professionals' and 'service users' (Napier and Fook, 2000: 218). Commonly the division many be between statutory and non-statutory workers, the latter being seen as powerless (Sim, 2000). Sometimes the 'powerful/powerless' dichotomy is between managers and frontline workers, and is also based on a more fundamental dichotomy which constructs the worker (self) as powerless and the 'other' as all powerful (Fook, 2004) (if speaking about the system or organisation in which the person works). Interestingly this binary is upended if talking about service users as 'the other', in which case the worker is constructed as powerful and the user as powerless. Nonetheless both sets of binaries are based on a similar construction.

Sometime the dichotomy may refer to styles of working i.e. an authoritative or more 'powerful' style of working cannot be combined with a more collegiate style.

2. The power of theory

An underlying assumption about theory is that it can be used (and is desirable for) controlling understanding and therefore controlling situations. This often leads to the assumption that theory can only be used in a rigid way (Napier and Fook, 2000: 217). This was the case for a very experienced social worker, who was also a very committed feminist, for whom feminist theory acted as a kind of a surety that she would not abuse her power. By seeing herself as a feminist, and by striving to work on a feminist theoretical framework, she saw herself as guarding against any accidental abuse of power. (See Fook, 2010)

These assumptions about the controlling power of theory are also related to the tendency to dichotomise 'theory vs practice', often leading practitioners to want to vacillate between prioritising theory or prioritising practice, not being able to conceptualise how each might complement each other in a fluid way. As a result, social workers often feel that they must 'choose sides' and either be good at practice or good at theory. This may also become an important part of their self-identity as professionals.

3. Power and possibilities for change

These sets of assumptions are related to assumptions about fatalism, a type of 'adjustment of the mind' to the inevitability of a situation (Fook, 2004: 22). They are also related to a person's self-identity and sense of agency, i.e. the extent to which they feel they are someone who has the ability to influence a situation. As mentioned earlier, they often involve dichotomous thinking ('I have no power'. . . 'they have all power'). Such assumptions were particularly the case in relation to frontline social workers and managers. Often people assume that even if they manage to bring about some change it will not be successful in the longer term, or will not be sustained. For example, powerful people will not listen to the change I want to make, or they will sabotage the change in some other way (Fook, 2004). Another problematic assumption is that the only proper change is total or structural change. Personal or small-scale change is devalued or dismissed (Fook, 2002).

4. *The power of discourse*

Many workers who critically reflect note how they uncover the operation of powerful discourses in their own assumptions. Tseris (2008) notes that although she was herself as very child-focused, how critical reflection revealed her work in child protection to be operating on an 'adult-centred' discourse, so that the situation was not seen or interpreted from the child's point of view.

Other workers note how the discourse of service users as powerless, may lead to erroneous assumptions about them which actually blind the worker to their power and also function to deny them any power (Cosier, 2008).

An interesting example is raised by Kicuroski (2008) who talks about how a female service user with a mental illness was characterised as 'emotionally dangerous' and therefore powerful. He was able to analyse this as a 'stigmatising discourse' and to see how it actually operated to deprive the woman of her rights.

In summary, most of these assumptions are reasonably predictable given the theoretical frameworks upon which critical reflection is based. However what is useful to note is that most people were not aware that these assumptions operated in their own practice. Whilst they could easily agree to the framework of analysis, it was a different experience to actually pinpoint the concrete way in which specific assumptions influenced their own practice.

In the following section I attempt to summarise some of the main ways in which practitioners reworked their assumptions about power.

Changes in thinking about power

Although all the changes discussed here relate to changes in thinking about power, I have categorised them in order to outline how notions of power underpin other aspects of thinking which influence practice. They cannot be separated out, and all contribute to a more complex understanding of social work practice. The changes that take place are categorised under four main headings:

1. New notions of power.
2. New notions of the self (as powerful).
3. New ways of practising.
4. New ways of thinking about theory.

1. New notions of power

The concept of power is reworked in a multitude of different ways, and is translated in many different ways into practice. Many people actually speak about their changed concept of power in Foucauldian terms i.e. *power is 'exercised not possessed'* (Fook and Gardner, 2007: 131). This means that power is seen as something which is dynamic, not finite, and has the potential to be used and interpreted in many different ways. This new way of conceptualising power often leads workers to be able to see how service users/clients, both as individuals and as a group, can also be powerful (Cosier, 2008: 56). This effectively frees users from being labelled as inherently 'powerless', and opens the way for more equal partnerships with professionals.

Broadly, related to the above idea of exercising (rather than possessing) power, people also talk about their notions of *power becoming more complex.* For example, Cosier (2008) speaks about an ability to acknowledge the many different factors contributing to power. Evans (2008: 7–9) talks about her realisation of how she exercised power unwittingly through her own decisions about what 'confidentiality' meant and how it should operate, so that even in believing that she was acting to preserve the power of the service user, she was still acting from a powerful position as a professional.

Others are able to incorporate an understanding of *contradictions involved in the operation of power* (Fook and Gardner, 2007: 131). Just as service users are not labelled as inherently powerless, people are also able to see that senior staff (such as managers) are not necessarily inherently powerful. Because power is a complex phenomenon, it can be exercised in a variety of ways, some of which may be contradictory, or work against each other.

Wieczorek (2008: 23) provides a fascinating example of an incident when a youthful service user proposed kissing her in exchange for doing something she asked. She discusses the contradictions this raised for her about both preserving boundaries (and power) whilst at the same time trying to be 'equal'. This led her to be more aware of how power is inextricably bound up with notions of professionalism.

Another set of changed thinking relates to an awareness of how power is embedded in particular ways of thinking, and how these ways of thinking may need to be changed in order to change the underlying operation of power. A prime example is the idea of certainty, or need for certainty, as described in Barbara's example earlier.

Some people speak of moving on from a concept of social workers empowering others (ie. people who need to be empowered, such as clients or service users) to the idea of working in an inclusive way (Napier and Fook, 2000: 222). The 'concept of empowering others therefore changes to a concept of 'working together', and the task becomes instead one of working together to create a shared environment or a shared position.

Interestingly, this new conception of power also results in a more open approach to understanding the perspective of service users and their experience (Redmond, 2004: 119–20; Cosier, 2008). Tseris (2008) illustrates this idea very effectively with her new principle for working in child protection. The critical reflection process resulted in her becoming aware of how child protection practice was based on an 'adult-centred' discourse. What she felt was needed as a result was a 'child-centred discourse of participation'. I include a large quote here to preserve the sense of what she sees this as:

> . . . 'child-centred' practice implies creating social justice outcomes for children in a broad sense, and can therefore incorporate the responsibility of social workers to pursue both protective and participatory practices. This means that I am not limited to a simplistic understanding of power as negative, inconsistent with social justice, and to be avoided when working with clients. In addition to being wholly unrealistic in an agency with statutory obligations, such an attempt to eschew power denies the possibility that power can be used in a productive way, to protect children and ensure minimum standards of care . . . therefore I am able to become clearer about the limitations of participation but also I am able to link the responsible use of power to creating social justice for children . . . helping and authority do not have to be seen as paradoxical or mutually exclusive.
>
> Tseris, 2008: 40

2. New notions of the self (as powerful)

Many people report becoming empowered themselves (see Fook and Askeland, 2006) for a full discussion of this). However it is interesting to note that this happens in many different ways, and it is more to do with reworking how they see themselves, seizing the power to construct their own identities, rather than gaining more power (in a simplistic sense). In other words, people learn how to create power by changing their own notions of themselves, rather than having power conferred from outside.

Some examples of the ways this happens are: 'writing my self back into the story' (Sim, 2000); being able to make a positive validation of yourself within a negative social environment (Fook, 2004: 23) and being able to recognise and value yourself (and therefore others) as a whole person/people (Fook, 2004: 23; Fook and Gardner, 2007: 131). This latter point is related to the idea that people also find a place for their emotions, which appears to be crucial in accepting themselves as people, as well as professionals. This change in thinking is therefore vital in helping people reconcile the often opposing expectations and boundaries between the 'personal' and 'professional' and clears the way for people to reconstruct an integrated identity. All the above changes contribute to an increased sense of personal agency (Schon, 1995: 224; Fook and Gardner, 2007: 131).

3. New ways of practising

Clearly some new ways of practising emerge from the above discussion, so I will include only a brief summary here. The ideas of 'sharing', working together, and participation, appear to replace former ideas of more hierarchical ways of empowering others. People may reframe empowering practice as being about creating a shared environment or position. Interestingly, this may carry over into new ideas about collegiality and connectedness with colleagues (Maich et al., 2000; Fook and Askeland, 2006: 51) and in fact enable better teamwork, or even inter-professional work, based on a better understanding of different colleagues' perspectives. Some people may in fact be better able to work with more senior colleagues, like managers.

On a very practical level, some people report being able to see more choices in terms of the actions they take (Fook and Askeland, 2006: 50). This may be because they have become aware of binary constructions which have limited their choices and gave a sense of 'forced choices'. Or it may be because they have become aware of the power of particular dominant discourses in shaping their choices and therefore an awareness of how 'one's choice of discourse can be a profound act of resistance' (Rubensohn, 2008: 90)

4. New ways of thinking about theory

As noted in the foregoing section, the process of critical reflection for many people uncovers key assumptions about the power of theory. In broad terms the changes in thinking associated with this mean that theory is seen more as a tool of the worker – it is something which can be used and interpreted, rather than something which has an independent life and authority. In this sense the changes are a little similar to some of the changes which take place in relation to the concept of power. That is, theory becomes seen as something which can be changed and created by social workers through their own experience, rather than something which rigidly rules or controls practice.

Specifically, some of the changes people report in relation to this involve a freeing up to integrate new theory into their practice (Fook and Gardner, 2007: 131) because they are able to interpret theory in relation to their own experience. This makes for a better ability to connect theory with their own experience, and this in itself is experienced as empowering.

Conclusion

How we conceptualise power is crucial to the practice of social work in many settings. Indeed the power of 'power' as a concept is incontrovertible. Because it underpins so many of our cultural and professional assumed ways of working, it is important to expose and examine these for their relevance in specific situations. The critical reflection model I have outlined in this chapter first discusses the theory of power used in the model, and also illustrates some actual conceptualisations of power which underlie many examples of social workers' practice. An analysis of social workers critical reflections on their practice reveals how many become aware of misconceptions about power embedded in their practice, and how they are able to change these conceptions in more complex ways. This provides a basis for changing practice in more complex ways which are more 'user-friendly', often opening up workers to different perspectives and experiences of all the range of colleagues and users they work with.

References

Agger, B. (1998) *Critical Social Theories.* Westview, Boulder.

Berlin, S. (1990) Dichotomous and Complex Thinking. *Social Service Review*, March: 46–59.

Boud, D., Keogh, R. and Walker, D. (Eds.) (1985) *Reflection: Turning Experience Into Learning.* Kogan Page, London.

Cosier, W. (2008) What Part of 'no' Don't You Understand? Social Work, Children and Consent. In Pockett, R. and Giles, R. (Eds.) *Critical Reflection: Generating Theory from Practice.* Sydney, Darlington Press.

Dewey, J. (1933). *How We Think: A Restatement of The Relation of Reflective Thinking to The Educative Process.* Boston, Heath.

Evans, M. (2008) When Worlds Collide: Understanding The Intersection of The Personal and Professional in Social Work Practice. In Pockett, R. and Giles, R. (Eds.) *Critical Reflection: Generating Theory from Practice.* Sydney, Darlington Press.

Fook. J. (1999) Reflexivity as Method. In Daly, J., Kellehear, A. and Willis, E. (Eds.) *Annual Review of Health Social Sciences*, la Trobe University.

Fook, J. (2002). *Social Work: Critical Theory and Practice.* London, Sage.

Fook, J. (2004) Critical Reflection and Transformative Possibilities. In Davies, L. and Leonard, P. (Eds.) *Scepticism/Emancipation: Social Work in a Corporate Era.* Avebury, Ashgate.

Fook, J. (2008) Forward. In Pockett, R. and Giles, R. (Eds.) *Critical Reflection: Generating Theory from Practice.* Sydney, Darlington Press.

Fook, J. (2010) Beyond Reflective Practice: Reworking The 'Critical' in Critical Reflection. In Bradbury, H. et al. (Eds.) *Beyond Reflective Practice: New Approaches to Professional Lifelong Learning*, London, Routledge.

Fook, J. and Askeland, G.A. (2006) The 'Critical' in Critical Reflection. In White, S. Fook, J. and Gardner, F. (Eds.) *Critical Reflection in Health and Social Care*. Maidenhead, Open University Press.

Fook, J. and Gardner, F. (2007) *Practising Critical Reflection; A Resource Handbook.* Open University Press, Maidenhead.

Kicuroski, T. (2008) Borderline Personality Disorder and Binary Thinking: Challenging Power Dynamics and Practice. In Pockett, R. and Giles, R. (Eds.) *Critical Reflection: Generating Theory from Practice*, Sydney, Darlington Press.

Maich, N.M., Brown, B. and Royle, J. (2000) Becoming Through Reflection and Professional Portfolios: The Voice of Growth in Nurses. *Reflective Practice*, 1: 3, 309–24.

Marcus, G.E. (1994) What Comes Just After 'Post'? The Case of Ethnography. In Denzin, N. and Lincoln, Y. (Eds.) *Handbook of Qualitative Research*, London, Sage.

Napier, L. and Fook, J. (2000) (Eds.) *Breakthroughs in Practice: Social Workers' Theorise Critical Moments.* London, Whiting and Birch.

Parton, N. (1994) Problematics of Government, (Post)Modernity and Social Work. *British Journal of Social Work*, 24: 9–32.

Pockett, R. and Giles, R. (2008) (Eds.) *Critical Reflection: Generating Theory from Practice*. Sydney, Darlington Press.

Redmond, B. (2004) *Reflection in Action*, Aldershot, Ashgate.

Rubensohn, R. (2008) International Social Work Versus Local Practice: The Moral Dilemma of Knowing Where to 'Give Aid'. In Pockett, R. and Giles, R. (Eds.) *Critical Reflection: Generating Theory from Practice*. Sydney, Darlington Press.

Rosaldo, R. (1993) *Culture and Truth*, London, Beacon Press.

Schon, D. (1983) *The Reflective Practitioner: How Professionals Think in Action*. New York: Basic Books.

Schon, D. (1995) Reflective Inquiry in Social Work Practice. In Hess, P. and Mullen, E.J. (Eds.) *Practitioner-Researcher Relationships*. San Fransisco, Jossey Bass.

Sim, S. (2000) They Took My Baby. In Napier, L. and Fook, J. (Eds.) *Breakthroughs in Practice: Social Workers' Theorise Critical Moments.* London, Whiting and Birch.

Steier, F. (1991) *Research and Reflexivity*, London, Sage.

Tseris, E. (2008) Examining These Words We Use: 'Participation', 'Empowerment' and The Child Protection Role. In Pockett, R. and Giles, R. (Eds.) *Critical Reflection: Generating Theory from Practice*. Sydney, Darlington Press.

Wieczorek, J. (2008) Crossing Invisible Lines; Professional Boundaries, Gender and Power in Social Work. In Pockett, R. and Giles, R. (Eds.) *Critical Reflection: Generating Theory from Practice*. Sydney, Darlington Press.

The art of social work practice

Edited by Toyin Okitikpi & Cathy Aymer

'It is rare to find a social work textbook that you can't put down, but this is one.' *Community Care*. 'Offers a "fresh look" at the approaches and methods used in social work . . . (The contributors) explore the role of social work and how it has been influenced by politics and society. They emphasise "the art of social work" and highlight the need for the profession to recapture the foundation of our work, which is based on the relationship with service users. This text is refreshing and thought provoking and would be beneficial to all involved in social work: practitioners, managers, students and educators. It is a book that you could refer to again and again and it would always have you thinking and reflecting. The book covers all the important areas of practice and acknowledges where mistakes have been made but, more importantly, offers sound guidance and advice on how we can improve and promote "the art of social work practice".' *Journal of Social Work*.

978-1-905541-30-0

Understanding interracial relationships

By Toyin Okitikpi

'Worryingly, the book confirms the continuation of racist thinking about race mixing and sexual liaisons between black and white. Small-scale qualitative studies can be extremely valuable and this one certainly is. I strongly recommend it.' *Adoption & Fostering*. 'I found myself nodding my head in agreement . . . seeks to understand many aspects of these relationships from the sexual attraction to the fears of rejection from nearest family to that of strangers . . . reveals that many people in interracial relationships are involved in innovative strategies which allow them to cope with the added demands that such a relationship still imposes in British society today.' *Well-being*.

978-1-905541-53-9

Working with children of mixed parentage

Edited by Toyin Okitikpi

'A compelling mix of research, theory and refreshing subjectivity.' *Children & Society*. 'What the reader will remember from this volume is the normality and resilience of children with one black and one white parent.' *Adoption & Fostering*. 'It also covers how to undertake direct work with children of mixed parentage.' *CAFCASS Practice and Research Digest*.

978-1-903855-64-5.

www.russellhouse.co.uk

Children's services at the crossroads
A critical evaluation of contemporary policy for practice

Edited by Patrick Ayre and Michael Preston-Shoot

'Access to the latest thinking from an impressive range of eminent academics (with a large array of practice experience).' *PSW*. **CONTENTS**: Children's services: reversing the vicious spiral *Patrick Ayre & Michael Preston-Shoot* **The policy context** Children and young people's policy in Wales *Ian Butler & Mark Drakeford* Safeguarding children: the Scottish perspective *Brigid Daniel & Norma Baldwin* The understanding systemic caseworker: the (changing) nature and meanings of working with children and families *Harry Ferguson* **Client group issues** The deprofessionalisation of child protection: regaining our bearings *Patrick Ayre & Martin Calder* New Labour and youth justice: what works or what's counted *John Pitts & Tim Bateman* Children in need: the challenge of prevention for social work *Kate Morris* Inadmissible evidence? New Labour and the education of children in care *Isabelle Brodie* **Research evidence on services** Looking after social work practice in its organisational context: neglected and disconcerting questions *Michael Preston-Shoot* Managerialism: at the tipping point? *Alex Chard & Patrick Ayre* Technology as magic: fetish and folly in the IT-enabled reform of children's services *David Wastell & Sue White* Playing with fire or rediscovering fire? The perils and potential for evidence based practice in child and family social work *Donald Forrester* For my next trick: illusion in children's social policy and practice *Michael Preston-Shoot & Patrick Ayre*.

978-1-905541-64-5

Managing child welfare and protection services

By Paul Harrison

'Combines an awareness of national policy with the necessity of managing resources both financial and human at a local level . . . a coherent analysis of the complexities of managing child welfare and protection services . . . outlines the particular moral challenges and dilemmas faced by managers . . . this book is well researched and thought-out and would provide any reader with food for thought as well as a useful reference tool for ideas and a guide to good practice.' *Rostrum*.

978-1-905541-52-2

www.russellhouse.co.uk

Social work assessment and intervention
Second edition
By Steven Walker and Chris Beckett

'The process of engaging in an assessment should be therapeutic and perceived of as part of the range of services offered.' This DOH view acknowledges that assessment is more than an administrative task, a form of gatekeeping for resources or a means of determining risk. It confirms the need for assessment and intervention to be conceptualised as part of a continuum of contact between social worker and service user. This essential book, acclaimed in its first edition, offers social workers an extensively revised, restructured and updated, comprehensive guide to empowering practice for them and the people with whom they work. Using case illustrations, evidence based guidance, and practical activities combined with extensive references, it

- is geared towards the needs of those on graduate training courses, PQ students, as well as for a range of in-service training in voluntary or statutory social work and social care
- combines the two practice elements of assessment and intervention in a unique integrated way consistent with anti-oppressive practice and the foundational values and skills of modern psycho-social practice
- addresses the need to deliver high quality care while managing the dilemmas presented by budget constraints.

978-1-905541-68-3

Crisis intervention
By Neil Thompson

'It is at times of crisis that the deepest pain is felt and the full intensity of human suffering can be experienced. It is also the point at which the potential for growth and enhancement is at its greatest.' *The author.* This clear and concise introduction to theory and methods shows the value of crisis intervention as an approach for anyone in the helping professions, and provides a foundation for further learning, so that its benefits for practice can be enhanced. An extensively revised and updated version of *Crisis Intervention Revisited* (Pepar, 1991), this book

- clears up misunderstandings and oversimplifications that have at times caused the immense value of crisis theory to have been lost
- takes fuller account of the sociological dimension of crisis, such as issues of discrimination on the grounds of gender, race/ethnicity, and age.

978-1-905541-67-6

Complaints panels in social care
By Catherine Williams and Katy Ferris

Aiming to enhance the work of panels for the benefit of all involved, this benchmark guide to complaints panels is built on the authors' many years' involvement in – and extensive research into – panels in several local authorities. Catherine Williams is an honorary Reader in Law at the University of Sheffield. She has written several articles on the subject of complaints. Katy Ferris is a Senior Lecturer in Law at Sheffield Hallam University and has worked as an Independent Panel Member and Chair.

978-1-905541-65-2

www.russellhouse.co.uk

Contemporary risk assessment in safeguarding children

Edited by Martin C. Calder

'The authors call for an evidence-based, comprehensive and equitable approach to risk assessment and teach the reader to produce risk management strategies where levels of intrusion are commensurate with levels of risk.' *ChildRIGHT*. 'Provides a lot of information . . . the topics are well presented and can be read in chapters or as a whole.' *Rostrum*. 'An absorbing and exciting read . . . A broad perspective of thinking about risk and the challenge of interpreting information gathered from and about children's lives . . . a good reference guide . . . extremely useful.' *Children & Young People Now*. 'Gems that will be a real boon to practice . . . tablets of wisdom set as a feast before you.' *PSW*.

978-1-905541-20-1

The carrot or the stick?
Towards effective practice with involuntary clients in safeguarding children work

Edited by Martin C. Calder

'Excellent material . . . on a subject that challenges all child care practitioners: how do we work with service users who don't want to work with us? The book ranges from the theoretical to the practical in responding to this question . . . a very useable framework for working with involuntary clients . . . would offer busy practitioners some useful tools.' *Community Care*. For work with children and young people, men and women, fathers and mothers in all relevant circumstances. 'The carefully selected chapters in this book offer systematic and evidence-based approaches.' *ChildRIGHT*. 'Relevant to practitioners, managers and planners. Accessible for students and teachers, the text is like effective practice – engaging, well structured, disciplined and encouraging.' *Rostrum*.

978-1-905541-22-5

Becoming ethical
A parallel, political journey with men who have abused

By Alan Jenkins

A practical guide for anyone who works in the field of interventions with men who have engaged in violence or sexual abuse towards partners and family members. It 'proposes a refreshing new perspective . . . It will definitely be added to my library of must have books.' *Addiction Today*. 'Intervention is seen in terms of power relations and practices within families and communities, and within the institutional, statutory and therapeutic settings in which men participate.' *ChildRIGHT*.
978-1-905541-40-9

www.russellhouse.co.uk